MW00873769

African Missionary Devotional Stories:
21 Inspirational Missionary Stories
Volume 2

African Missionary Devotional Stories Volume 2
by Stephen Kuert

This book or parts thereof may not be reproduced in any form, stored in a retrieval system or transmitted in any form by any means—electronic, mechanical, photocopy, recording or otherwise—without prior written permission of the author, except as provided by United States of America copyright law.

© 2015 by Stephen Kuert
All rights reserved

Thank you to Edith Kaiser for being willing to edit this book.

Foreword for Volume 2

   The book in your hands is the second part of African Missionary Devotional Stories. The first volume contained 21 true stories about lives being impacted by the Lord through simple obedience. This book contains the same. Over the past ten years I've had multiple people tell me that I needed to put into writing some of the stories from my experience in Africa as a missionary.

   It has been an amazing journey of partnership with the Lord. He has used my life in some incredible ways in several nations across East Africa as well as here in the United States. My prayer is that as you read this book you will experience a fresh surge of faith for God to use your life to impact the nations.

I believe that missions is the mission of God. Our responsibility as Christ followers is to partner with His mission. The more we identify with the mission of God the more missions becomes our focus. In other words, if we desire to know God's mission then we must have a vision for missions. The really neat aspect of God's mission is that it is incredibly personal.

Jesus comes to earth to embody the mission of God in order to launch worldwide missions in order to make God's mission known. Our response to God's mission requires no less—personal involvement. Stated another way missions thrives when God's people embrace God's mission. Missions dies when God's people embrace other missions. It's pretty simple. Yet, incredibly tricky to implement. There are just so many other competing missions in this world. Hence, missions become a secondary pursuit leaving the nations of the world oblivious to God's ultimate mission in the person of Christ Jesus.

Even for people who have responded to God's Mission it is very easy to become distracted; there is a perpetual pull away from missions. We easily focus on secondary matters neglecting the primary. How can we remedy this situation? I think it goes back to the etymology of the word 'mission'. Originally, it is a Latin word—*Missio.* It signifies being sent. It involves the idea of a commission from someone with the authority to bestow it.

This is where we get the idea of the Great Commission in Matthew 28. Jesus tells His disciples: "*All authority in heaven and on earth has been given to me—therefore, GO into all the world and make disciples of all the nations.*" It's a powerful charge. It's action-oriented. It's partnership demanding a specific response. Disciples are invited to partner with Christ in making more disciples among all the *ethne*—ethnic groups. Our response to His commission is to make ourselves available to be sent.

To me this means that we have to keep our hearts centered on the identity of the One doing the sending. Jesus has all authority. Jesus desires the nations to be discipled in the knowledge of His ways and heart. He looks for people to send in order to cooperate with Him in this endeavor. It's His Mission becoming missions through the lives of people being sent.

God's Mission plus people being willing to receive a co-*Missio* equals missions. Is this more than just a play on words? Yes, I believe so. As we embrace God's Mission our lives receive purpose and divine destiny. We become ambassadors of the Mission of God by partnering with Jesus in doing missions. People are changed in the discipleship process to know and love Him. This in turn qualifies them to respond to God's mission by partnering with heaven in a fresh expression of missions.

When I was fourteen years old I had the privilege of vacationing for ten days on Kenya's coast with the late Dr. John York, author of *Missio Dei.* It was an unforgettable experience. The man permeated God's Mission—his prayers, his conversation, his passion for God, and his love for people. He was all about making Jesus known—the reality of discipleship. I remember multiple staff at the hotel where we stayed approaching him for prayer before we left. Others, many of who were Muslims, wanted to know more about Christ. He shared with them with such gentleness and compassion. Tears would often flow down his face. Missions was his lifestyle everywhere he went—even on vacation. I had never seen anything so remarkable and so attractive.

This devotional is a simple reminder of what happens when simple people embody God's Mission in the pursuit of missions. I pray that you will be inspired, challenged, convicted, and consumed with Heaven's Mission—the revelation of Jesus Christ to the nations in this generation. This is a massive undertaking, one that will require singular focus. One that will require your participation. May your heart be stirred to connect your time, finances, families, friends and resources to heaven's ultimate purpose—God's Mission.

Table of Contents:

Day 1: An Example in This Generation

Quote of the Day: Someone asked, will the heathen who have never heard the Gospel be saved? It is more a question with me whether we — who have the Gospel and fail to give it to those who have not — can be saved. - *Charles Spurgeon*

Verse of the Day: Let no one despise or think less of you because of your youth, but be an example (pattern) for the believers in speech, in conduct, in love, in faith, and in purity. I Timothy 4:12

Young Christians in Action (Y.C.A.) is a university group we formed in Antanarivo, Madagascar. College students from across the city have the opportunity to participate in a community of young adults that meets at least once a week. This includes praise and worship, prayer, Bible discussion, and food. For a period of time we met at the Bible Society League building near the downtown area with spectacular views of Antanarivo.

We were in a series called "*Tupos*" based on 1 Timothy 4:12. *Tupos* is the Greek for example or model. Paul tells Timothy, the young pastor, that he is called to be an example to the believers in five ways: in speech, conduct, love, faith, and purity. It's quite a challenge.

We spent several weeks examining each aspect of Paul's admonishment. I encouraged the Y.C.A. students to invite their friends. One particular afternoon, a young man walked into the meeting room as I was sharing on purity. He left prior to meeting him. The following week he reappeared and sat enthralled throughout the gathering. At several points, there were tears in his eyes.

Afterwards, he asked if we could meet at a later point during the week. We set up a time and I asked the friend who had invited him to come along. We met as planned. It was a cordial interaction. He shared his story: upbringing in a denominational church that was totally lifeless, a tight-knit family, education in Belgium, and a desire to pursue ecology on the Big Island. His French was impeccable. I felt drawn to him.

He shifted his weight and wondered if we could continue discussing purity. His friend asked to be excused. The young man shared in greater depth his experience in a very sensual Belgian culture. Tears began coursing down his face. It had been painful on many different levels.

He knew his lifestyle didn't please God and it was clear that he had been under heavy conviction. I shared on the restorative nature of the Gospel and the sustaining power of the Holy Spirit in the life of a believer. Years in church had never afforded him the chance to hear about either. God was clearly at work.

I asked if we could pray together. He quietly nodded. We prayed a prayer of repentance together. Suddenly, I felt impressed that we needed to ask his friend to come pray with us. *"Would that be okay?"* I asked this young man.

He hesitated slightly before nodding.

I went outside and called our mutual friend back inside. *"We are going to pray together; God wants to bring healing to your friend's life."*

At first it was a bit awkward, but soon God's presence removed any kind of tension. As we prayed this dear young man began to weep uncontrollably. He soon crumpled out of the couch onto the floor. There was a puddle of tears on the wooden floor. It was so beautiful to see genuine repentance and restoration taking place in my living room. Close to half an hour later this young man walked out of the front door of Trade Bois no 15 transformed—forever.

Over the years we have become best of friends. God has moved marvelously in this young man's life. Many lives have been touched through his surrender to Christ that day. Several months later his church officially excommunicated him for casting devils out of youth group members who needed deliverance. Many surrendered their lives to Christ.

What can you expect from someone who has come face to face with the purity and holiness of Jesus? He has become an example in this generation. His life is a reminder of the power of Christ's grace. God has given him a platform of influence in this generation.

Question of the Day: Are you living your life as a *tupos*—a model or example to this generation? In what areas do you need to grow in order to implement Paul's instructions to Timothy in 1 Timothy 4:12?

Musings: It has been said that the United States has more exposure to the Word of God than any other nation in history. Christian book stores, podcasts, Bible apps, devotional apps, churches on every street corner, television stations, hundreds of Bible translations, etc… With so much access and exposure to the Word of God one must ask the question—why is our nation not any different?

In my opinion, the simple answer is obedience. We seek out new teachings and revelations while forgetting to obey the simple truths that would really transform us. One of my favorite preachers says this: "Obedience is God's excuse to bless you."

I don't know about you, but I want to live a blessed a life (James 1:25). I think one of the greatest ways in which He blesses us is by giving us influence to impact other people's lives. He makes us examples of His grace, testimonies of His mercy, and demonstrations of His power. I've found that unbelievers have a hard time arguing against such real life experience.

Obedience in these five areas: speech, conduct, love, faith, and purity develops a life of integrity. People take note at this kind of life. This creates influence. Jesus desires to make our lives examples in this generation.

Day 2: Jesus and Coffee

Quote of the Day: Tell the students to give up their small ambitions and come eastward to preach the gospel of Christ.- *Francis Xavier*

Verse of the Day: Out of the same mouth come forth blessing and cursing. These things, my brethren, ought not to be so. Does a fountain send forth simultaneously from the same opening fresh water and bitter water? James 3:10-11.

I pulled up to the petrol station to fill up. I was quite tired after preaching two services earlier that Sunday morning. More than that I was weary from the strain of life. My wife, Bailey, had been sick for several months. I found myself alone in church and at the petrol station due to a recent medical procedure. Speaking that morning had been difficult; I battled doubt and feelings of discouragement. Amazingly, God had used the message to bring ten young people to salvation.

As David, the young fuel attendant fueled up my car I noticed that his right eye was totally clouded over. I knew how desperately Bailey needed healing so I offered to pray for his eye despite battling my own feelings. He accepted readily. Nothing happened.

Over the ensuing weeks David and I became friends. Every time I needed fuel I would head to this particular gas station to find David. I visited David and Pamela in their little one bedroom apartment on the complete other side of town. They were touched that I would be willing to do so saying that I was the first pastor/missionary and first mzungu (white person) to ever visit them in their little one bedroom apartment.

One day some months later Bailey and I were at the same petrol station where David and I had first met. As I pulled up my vehicle to be fueled, the young man made a beeline for us.

"Hey Steve, how are you? Do you remember what we prayed about the first time we met?" he asked directly.

Of course, I remembered. The glossed over lens on his retina was a continual reminder to me. Glancing up I noticed that his eye was clear again. Before I could ask, he continued the story.

"Last week, I heard about a free medical clinic. The eye surgeon there said I needed a surgery." It had been several days since I had last seen him.

"Go on," I waited impatiently.

"I was told to go to the eye clinic two days later. There the surgeon performed an operation that would have

cost 65,000 shillings for free. Two days later my sight was restored."

I couldn't believe my ears. I had sincerely prayed more out of concern rather than expectation. In other words, it was kind of a prayer rather than a faith for a miracle prayer if that makes sense. Yet, God had answered in a most unusual way.

"God has answered your prayer," His face beamed with genuine enthusiasm.

Bailey and I were so encouraged to hear his testimony. Our health challenges had at times even caused us to doubt our prayers. We had experienced so much confusion. Yet, here was a clear and direct answer to a very simple prayer with a very clear message to me, *"God hears your prayers and answers your prayers Stephen Kuert."*

As I reflected on what had happened, I felt a prompting in my heart to ask David about his need for salvation. However, he was working and it would be difficult to get undistracted time with him.

We arranged to meet for coffee some time later. All four members of the Ochieng family were present and accounted for: David, Pamela, and their two children, Ashley, and baby Brilliant. David's eye had improved to almost perfect condition. Pamela nursed the young baby.

"I would like to ask you guys something."

"Go ahead," David nodded.

"Have you ever surrendered your lives to Jesus? I think you have seen how much He loves you."

David nodded in the affirmative. He had surrendered his life to Christ many years ago as a teenager, but struggled to live it out. Pamela looked away. I could tell that there was a battle inside of her.

"Could I pray with you to receive Christ?" I asked Pamela. *"And pray for strength for your family to follow Christ?"* I asked David.

They both nodded as Pamela continued to breast-feed the baby.

In the middle of a Java House on the north side of Nairobi, we prayed together to receive Christ. It was awesome to see an entire family making a commitment to follow Christ. Relationship is the bridge on which divine transactions take place. Sometimes we just have to step out and build the relationship even when we don't feel like it.

Question of the Day: When you are discouraged how can you find ways to minister to others? How can you make yourself available even when you don't feel it?

Musings: My mouth is the thermometer of my heart. Far too often I find my mouth saying things that I wish it wouldn't. What comes out usually determines my attitude and perception of the day. When it comes to ministering to other people it is critical that my mouth doesn't destroy the relationship and sabotage my God-given influence.

In such moments, I need a "heart-check". I've learned to sit quietly before the Lord and ask Him to show me why I reacted in a certain way or why certain things came out of me. I'm usually amazed at the answer. Sometimes, there are fears inside of me that I hadn't identified, or deep-seated identity issues that need to be addressed, or anger and unforgiveness towards someone, or some kind of evil influence that I allowed to pass through my eye/ear gates into my heart. The list is virtually endless.

As I'm intentional to allow Him to correct the issue in my heart by acknowledging it and surrendering it, I find that my overall sense of "*peace*" returns. I'm then able to interact with people without feeling like my mouth is going to betray me. This allows the Lord to use our lives to build bridges with people to see the glory of Christ in and through us.

Day 3: Don't Drown Now

Quote of the Day: The Christian is not obedient unless he is doing all in his power to send the Gospel to the heathen world.- *A. B. Simpson*

Verse of the Day: Who are being guarded and garrisoned by God's power through your faith till you fully inherit that final salvation that is ready to be revealed for you in the last time. I Peter 1:5

Sach invited me to go swimming. I had been living in the US for a couple of years pursuing my graduate studies. I'm not much of a cold weather person so I decided to head back to Kenya for the Christmas holidays to see my parents and reconnect with my Kenyan friends. After several days on the ground of intensive leadership meetings, Sach decided that I needed some much-needed R&R.

I agreed completely. *"Let's go swimming,"* came his enthusiastic response.

"We can invite our friends from all over my neighborhood to come along," he added.

It was a great idea except for one crucial element—I knew no one in Kenya with a pool.

"We will go to the National Athletic Stadium." Problem solved thanks to some quick thinking.

After a few phone calls and text messages, we assembled a group of about ten people together for the purpose of a Kenyan swim party.

The admission fee cost hardly anything and after a rather long walk we stood before an Olympic size pool complete with a 30-meter high dive. My first thought was to make sure that everyone knew how to swim. Sure enough, all but one guy had learned how to do the doggie paddle.

The non-swimmer promised to hang out in the shallow end and watch our personal effects so that no one helped themselves to our belongings. The place was packed with other swimmers taking advantage of the public facilities. After several hours of having fun in the water, I was tired and felt that it was time to pack up and call it a day. I headed for a final swim in the deep end.

As I neared the far edge of the pool, I heard Sach and a couple of the other guys crying out, *"He's drowning! Save him!"*

At first I thought that they were talking about me because I couldn't see anyone else where they were pointing. *"Hurry! He won't make it."*

I caught a glimpse of a frenzied hand motion of someone's flailing arms beneath the surface of the water. Oh my goodness, someone was drowning and just a few meters away from me. I hadn't seen this guy get in and I certainly hadn't seen him go under.

Splash! Splash! My friends had dived into water and soon had the sputtering, coughing, and wheezing young man back on the edge of the pool. After a few moments of regurgitating chlorine, he finally regained his strength.

Asanteni! (Thank you) he finally managed.

"Do you know how to swim?" one of my friends asked him.

"No, not at all," he answered.

"Then why did you jump into the deep end?" the whole group asked in disbelief.

"I didn't realize it was the deep-end," he stammered. Clearly, he had no idea of just how real the danger of drowning can be when someone doesn't know how to swim.

Sach seized the opportunity to share Christ with the bewildered young man. There was no need to convince him of the reality of death. He had escaped by a few seconds.

"Are you ready to face the judgment seat my friend?" Sach continued.

A few moments later he knelt in prayer next to the very spot where he had almost drowned a moment earlier. I had the privilege of leading this young man in a prayer of repentance to receive Christ as His Lord and Savior.

The whole incident lasted less than ten minutes. I kept thinking to myself, *"What would have happened if we hadn't been there?" "Would someone else have pulled him out?" "Would he have entered eternity without Christ?"*

The difference between life and death for this young man was quite literally a few seconds and a couple of people willing to dive in after him.

I have also contemplated God's protection. It would be so easy to fall into the deep-end so to speak in so many different areas of life. This world can be a really dangerous place without His Hand of mercy keeping us from harm's way.

Being in the right place at the right time is essential to both of these ideas. Jesus positions us for service; He also positions us for divine protection. Our response is to be ready and obedient. We never know when someone is going to stumble into the deep-end and need our help.

Questions of the Day: Have you experienced God's positioning in your life? How do you best cooperate with Him in this process? What is your biggest challenge?

Musings: My biggest challenge is fear. People who know me and the crazy places that I've lived in Africa sometimes ask the question: *"Don't you ever get afraid?"* The simple answer is: *"Of course."*

I've been in several riots, had thieves jump into my car at night, experienced a grenade explode outside my front gate, lived in a war-torn country where the rebels shelled the city for fun on the weekends, had bullets shot over my head, spent extended periods of time with dangerous criminals, fallen ill for lengthy periods of time for inexplicable reasons, etc…

Of course, I've felt afraid sometimes. Who wouldn't? However, I've never walked in fear for any length of time. Being afraid is a normal human emotion that accompanies danger. Walking in fear is a spiritual attack.

Walking in fear is the devil's trick intended to provoke anxiety, panic, and deeper-seated issues of abandonment, isolation, and unbelief. One is an emotional response that can be overcome quickly. The other is a spiritual paralysis that will suck the faith out of your soul.

At the end of the day, the issue really isn't safety; it's obedience. For years, I have clung to the truth that the safest place in the world to be is in the will of God. The will of God doesn't imply that nothing bad will ever happen to us or that we will never go anywhere dangerous. Rather, it guarantees at least three things.

First, that He will be with us in each and every situation no matter what is going on. Second, that He will give us the grace to continue experiencing His divine peace regardless of what happens. And third, that He will use the situation for His glory and our ultimate good (Rom 8:28). This has been the case in every challenge, every robbery, every attack, every illness, every distress, and every false accusation that I have faced.

Interestingly, some of the best sleep I've ever experienced has been during full on rebel attacks when machine gun rounds were being discharged just down the street. Why? I was in His will. I had perfect peace that nothing would happen to me unless it was in His purpose for my life. And as I listened for His voice, I knew that I would be protected. So I slept—deeply and soundly.

Are you in His will today? That's a question that only you can answer. If you are, relax; all will be well, even if it doesn't make any sense at all in this current moment. If you aren't in His will now would be a great time to get your heart right and ask Him to reposition you.

Day 4: The Run-Away

Quote of the Day: We talk of the Second Coming; half the world has never heard of the first- *Oswald J. Smith*

Verse of the Day: "Withstand him; be firm in faith against his onset—rooted, established, strong, immovable, and determined, knowing that the same identical sufferings are appointed to your brotherhood (the whole body of Christians) throughout the world. I Peter 5:9

Derek randomly showed up at church one day to ask for help. At fifteen years old life can be very challenging, especially in an African capital city boasting millions of people. He was confused, disoriented, and hungry. Sach and I sat and listened quietly as he poured out his hurting heart.

Running away from home sounded like a great idea, a week previous. Real life contradicted the fanciful notion. No friends, no money, no connections, and no lodging have a funny way of putting things back into perspective—very quickly.

Now, Derek's simple desire was to return home. He wanted money to buy a bus ticket to return to his family. From what we could gather, the young man had run away from home because he was tired of being forced to go to a boarding school and because his relationship with his uncle and aunt, the people who took care of him wasn't the best.

Sach had a better idea, *"Steve, what if we take him home?"*

"Home?" I gaffed.

"Yes, we could use your car," Sach replied.

"All the way back to Maragua?" I asked again.

I had never been to Maragua before and the very name sounded like it was a long ways away. Plus, I didn't really want to drive all that way only to get involved in a domestic affair that really was none of my business. We had just met this young man and had no idea if he was even telling us the truth.

"It's not that far at all," came the reply I anticipated.

Since the first day that I met him, Sach has had a way of stretching me far beyond my normal comfort zone. God uses him to expand me and challenge me, pulling things out of me that sometimes I didn't know were there. I nodded my head in assent even as I wondered how we could know if Derek was being straight-forward with us.

Derek had randomly showed up at church because he believed that Christians would help him. This was our golden opportunity to prove his expectations. Sach and I have often talked about the power of the church in crisis moments. It was an opportunity to shine.

We agreed to take him home on a Saturday when we would have the best chance of finding his family home. Our condition was that he had to ask his surrogate family to forgive him for running away without giving them a hint of where he had gone. Humility is never easy at fifteen. However, he assured us that he had learned his lesson and was willing to do so.

We felt strongly to share about the Prodigal Son. Disconnected and cut off from everything and everyone he wasted his life away. He listened attentively as we took turns encouraging him to learn from this profligate's mistakes by making the decision to receive the Father's affection, identity, and authority. Derek didn't need to make a total mess of his life.

The words seemed to ring true in his current experience as he made the simple decision to receive Christ's forgiveness. As we sped down the highway towards Maragua Derek's face seemed much lighter then when I had first met him.

Just over an hour later we pulled into the small town of Maragua. Derek directed us to his uncle's house. We parked the car and hiked up a small hill to reach the small stone structure with corrugated iron roofing sheets. We walked up to the small door and knocked. It opened as a middle-aged gentleman emerged.

"Hello sir! We've brought Derek back home," we stated.

"Who are you?" came the uncle's terse response.

"I am a pastor," Sach replied.

"I am a missionary," I answered.

The aunt and a cousin now stood with the uncle as they invited us into their home to have a seat in the living room.

"A pastor and a missionary have brought Derek back to my house?" marveled the middle-aged farmer. He was clearly in disbelief that this was happening. Many East Africans hold pastors and missionaries in high esteem.

"Derek would like to say something," Sach added.

Slowly, but methodically Derek shared his story—how he ran away, why he ran away, how he met us, his decision to receive Christ, and his desire for forgiveness.

The aunt and uncle were speechless. All tension quickly evaporated. Forgiveness soon swept across the room.

They had been too harsh, too demanding, too reserved in their affection. Derek would be welcomed back into the family with open arms. He would be given a fresh start.

After sharing a cup of *chai* we said our farewells, jumped into the car and headed back to. A relationship had been healed. A family was restored. And a spiritual connection had been established between Derek and his family as well as between Derek and us. This is the power of genuine forgiveness.

Question of the Day: How are you connected to other believers in your life? What can you do to include them in your spiritual battles? How can you overcome the tendency to be a spiritual loner?

Musings: I've been truly blessed in my life to have amazing friends who have walked with me through some very dark days. This wasn't always the case. I was convinced during my first year of university that I could make it all alone. I just couldn't understand why I kept falling flat on my face spiritually speaking. I was so weak, but refused to admit it.

The Lord painstakingly revealed my pride as well as the fear of rejection that kept me isolated from experiencing fellowship with others. I will never forget the day a team of prophetically gifted and incredibly discerning people walked me through deliverance from rejection once and for all. My life was transformed. From that moment on, I began to pray for solid friendships. God continues to answer those prayers even ten years later! I have found such strength and encouragement from these divine connections.

Mark records the story of a certain paralytic who is let down at Jesus' feet through the roof of a crowded house. In my opinion, the real heroes of the story are the unnamed friends who picked the guy up, carried him up on the roof, tore through the ceiling, and held the rope as he was positioned to receive his miracle. Without such friends there is no breakthrough.

God has given me at least four such individuals. They have walked me through many dark moments of the soul. We pray, share, talk, dream, joke, encourage, and challenge one another, mostly from afar. They are my brothers and true friends who have held the rope for me.

Who are yours? Could this be the day you let God heal your heart so that you can experience the strength and safety that comes from other believers?

Day 5: Piki-piki Pile-Up

Quote of the Day: The mark of a great church is not its seating capacity, but its sending capacity-
Mike Stachura

Verse of the Day: "Fear not as there is nothing to fear, for I am with you; do not look around you in terror and be dismayed, for I am your God. I will strengthen and harden you to difficulties, yes, I will help you; yes, I will hold you up and retain you with My victorious right hand of rightness and justice." Isaiah 41:10

A South African in our church in Dar owned a small car and a piki-piki (Swahili for motorbike). It was nothing fancy, just a 100cc dirt bike. He had decided to sell everything off and return to South Africa for good. He stopped by my house one day somewhat unexpectedly.

"*I'm off to South Africa,*" he stated.

"*When will you be back?*" I answered.

"*No plans as of yet,*" he replied.

"*I want to talk to you about my car and piki-piki.*"

"What about them?" I asked unsure of his question.

"Can I keep them here?" I sort of stammered for an answer.

Oh, and could you try and sell them for me? he continued before I could find an answer.

"For how much?" I asked still unsure if I had agreed to his first question let alone the second.

"Whatever is reasonable. You can take a percentage for the church."

That was the last time I ever saw this man—I guess he figured that a missionary pastor could be trusted.

I had no idea how to sell either in a place like Tanzania, especially when they weren't mine. Neither vehicle had insurance nor had the back taxes been paid for registration after a little further investigation.

The whole scenario increasingly felt kind of shady so I decided to get my friend Muddy involved in the process. He is a savvy Tanzanian with street smarts and could hopefully find a quick buyer. Hopefully, he would be able to sell them quickly, pay off the government taxes, generate some income for Muddy, and send the rest of the money back to South Africa.

"Can you sell them?" I asked hesitantly.

"Very easily," he replied.

"Can I use the piki until it is sold?" he beamed.

"There's no insurance and the registration is expired," I added.

"No problem," he countered.
"It's not my bike," I stammered.

"Whose is it?"
"Umm…long story."

With that I allowed myself to be talked into an even unwise situation. The plan went well for the first few days. Muddy rode the motorcycle to and fro looking for potential buyers. Many were interested; few were willing to deal with the registration issues.

One day my phone rang—it was Muddy's number, but not his voice.

"Your boy has been hit. We threw him into the back of a car…" Click. The line cut out. Obviously, Muddy's line didn't have any more credit. I quickly called back.

"Who is this?" I asked wondering if someone had stolen Muddy's phone.

"Muddy is in serious condition. The pik-piki was hit by a truck—he was thrown through the air into a ditch. He's in the back of a car being rushed to the hospital." My heart sank.

Just the day before Muddy and I had talked about the protection that is available to us as believers. As a MBB, he had experienced several threats since receiving Christ and lived under a continual cloud of fear.

I couldn't believe this was happening, nor how foolish I had been to actually let him take the piki-piki. Where was the protection of God we had talked about and prayed about the day before? How ironic that the accident had taken place the day after our conversation. The timing was unbelievable. I jumped in my vehicle and drove at break neck speeds through the streets of Dar.

Arriving at the hospital, I watched Muddy being placed on a stretcher. He was delirious. He saw me for a brief moment and called out: *"Stevu, Stevu, I'm scared,"* The medical team whisked him away.

The Good-Samaritans who had rescued him and called me on the phone stood nearby. "*My name is Abdullah, but you can call me White.*"

"*Abdu…. I mean…White, it's nice to meet you. I'm Steve. Thank you for helping Muddy.*"

"*No problem. He kept shouting your name after he was hit. So I picked up his cell phone and dialed your number.*"

With that began one of the most interesting turn of events I've ever experienced. Amazingly, Muddy only had a slight abrasion on his forearm, and an open lesion on his leg. The helmet he was wearing was split in two, but he was okay. A few stitches later he was released to hobble out of the hospital on crutches.

The doctor remarked that he was very fortunate to be alive—let alone not to have broken bones! His body recovered rather well and he was able to report back to work a week later. God had protected him after all!

Question of the Day: When have you been aware of Christ's protection in your life this past month? How did you respond in that situation?

Musings: This story still amazes me. There are so many things that come to mind. Divine protection is so real! What I didn't mention in the story is that the reason Muddy came to see me the day before the accident is that he received an Islamic death threat written in Arabic called 'Al-Badri'. Someone snuck into his apartment and put the small piece of paper in his living room. Yeah, I know it sounds weird. Believe me I didn't know what to make of it either. The day before the accident he had been distraught telling me that his life would soon be over because he had found the little scroll in his sofa. We talked at length; I shared the Word of God and we prayed together fervently asking for protection.

Within 24 hours my cell rang with the news that completely stupefied me. This experience taught me first-hand that curses in Africa are no small matter. I'm so thankful that Jesus prevailed in that situation. At first I was mystified at the whole experience. In sharing the story with two of my most trusted Tanzanian brothers in Christ, they both offered the same insight. *"Muddy, walked away with only scratches. Jesus is far greater than every curse."*

I learned two important things: First, the power of the name of Christ. I've often watched in amazement, as African pastors cast out demons from people during the church service. At the mention of the name of Jesus the possessed person will go crazy often flailing on the floor.

A seasoned missionary once told me that this is because the devil hates the name of Jesus more than anything else on planet earth. As such I've found that one of the most effective ways to pray about protection in my life is to sing, pray, whisper, meditate, or confess His beautiful name.

The second thing I learned is that to defeat the devil we need to declare the Word of God. Remember Jesus in the wilderness? Three times the enemy came. Three times Jesus resisted in the same way: "*It is written.*" If Jesus, the Son of God, needed to know the word to overcome the enemy what does that say to us?

A combination of the name of Jesus and His Word is sure to send the enemy fleeing. These are our spiritual weapons. We must learn to use them in order to ward off each and every attack of the enemy.

Day 6: Piki-Piki Pile-Up Part II

Quote of the Day: The spirit of Christ is the spirit of missions. The nearer we get to Him, the more intensely missionary we become- *Henry Martyn*

Verse of the Day: "And God's peace shall be yours, that tranquil state of a soul assured of its salvation through Christ, and so fearing nothing from God and being content with its earthly lot of whatever sort that is, that peace which transcends all understanding shall garrison and mount guard over your hearts and minds in Christ Jesus. Philippians 4:7

As soon as I was sure that Muddy was receiving proper medical care I headed to the site of the accident. White accompanied me. I kept thinking that the guy would ask for money for being willing to help Muddy. I had jumped to an unfounded conclusion. In fact, he never asked. The piki-piki had been impounded by the police, as had the truck. Both were being held down the road at the Oyster Bay Police Station.

I explained to White that the motorcycle wasn't insured. *"No problem. The truck hit your piki-piki."*

"Umm…it's not really my piki-piki. It belongs to a 'friend' in South Africa," I countered.

"That won't be an issue. The registration will indicate the real owner."

"Umm..the registration isn't up to date," I stuttered.

"We can take care of that easily," he offered.

"Umm…the taxes haven't been pain," I had a sinking feeling in my stomach.

He laughed, *"Come on. I can help you."* The sun had just started to set as dusk covered the bustling seaside city.

Arriving at the police station, I was escorted into a little room with several Tanzanian cops as well as a group of young men. A single light bulb illuminated the room. I felt rather intimidated—and very grateful to have White with me. This was certainly not how I envisioned spending my evening. Where was the Lord in all of this craziness?

The cop jumped into legal proceedings—the vehicles were impounded, there would be hauling fees, lock-up fees, storage fees, investigative fees, attorney fees, court fees, settlement fees, etc.. He was talking so fast in Dar Street Swahili that I could hardly keep up. Surely it couldn't be that complicated could it?

He paused and looked at all of us. "*I know that this will cost a fortune and require much time to settle. So I want all of you go outside and discuss the best way forward.*"

Was he serious? I reluctantly followed White as he joined the group of young men headed towards the big tree in the police station courtyard.

"*The driver of the vehicle is here.*" White whispered.

"*How do you know?*" I asked.

"*It's the only reason so many guys would have come out. They want to protect his identity from us and from the cops. Let me do the talking.*"

"*Umm...okay,*" I nodded. I sensed the peace of the Lord.

The Street Slang Swahili exploded fast and furious. It was hard to catch it all. I could tell that White was threatening the group with how many connections I had as an important American and how they would all be locked up for concealing the truth. Obviously, they knew nothing of the registration/insurance issues that would have greatly hindered my case.

"We need an agreement," he asserted.

One of the young men, named Gilbert agreed. *"We will pay to have the piki-piki fixed if you will agree not to press charges."*

"And?" White countered.

"We will cover the medical costs today for the driver."

"And?" White was ruthless.

"And... we agree to split the police costs 50-50 to drop the case right here and now."

"Done," answered my impromptu negotiator.

The sense of peace increased. I knew that this guy was a Godsend. I would have had no chance of negotiating this on my own.

We walked back into the police station. White stated to the cops that we would settle without a legal proceeding. The cop smiled and handed us an envelope. We each contributed a rather hefty amount of money to cover "police fees".

We drafted a contract in the parking lot that both Gilbert and myself signed and I was given a copy of his National ID card as a guarantee. We loaded the piki-piki into the back of the pick-up truck. White assured me that he knew these guys and all would be well.

Again a peace swept over me.

To make a long story short, Gilbert repaired the motorcycle. Muddy fully recovered. We never sold the piki-piki. A pastor from Congo showed up one day saying that the South African brother had promised it to him. After a phone call to Cape Town, I gladly turned it over to him—glad to be rid of it. I built a friendship with both Gilbert and White for the remainder of my time in Tanzania. We often talked about Jesus and His great love for the people of Tanzania.

On several occasions they both attended the Ocean International Community Church where I served as the pastor. To the best of my knowledge neither ever made a decision to follow Christ, at least not yet. Who knows how the story will finally turn out?

Question of the Day: How quick are you to jump to conclusions about certain "facts"? Have you taken time to listen for His perspective in a given situation? What could the Lord be teaching you in your current stressful situation about His peace?

Musings: Finding the voice of God in a stressful situation can be tough. He is speaking, but so are many other voices. There are at least three other voices that complicate our capacity to hear the Lord's voice. The first is the voice of the enemy—trying to accuse, condemn, and confuse. Secondly, there is the voice of our flesh—crying out for self-interests and personal rights to prevail. And lastly, there is the voice of others—attempting to give us their personal advice and direction.

In order, to find the voice of the Lord in a certain situation I use the "peace rule". This rule allows God's peace to be the "referee" of my heart. Basically, referees arbitrate what should and shouldn't take place in a sporting match or athletic competition. In the same way, the voice of the Lord will produce peace in our hearts regarding what is or isn't of Him. No matter how good something may seem if there is no peace in your heart then it isn't of Him.

Sound too simple? Try it. You will be amazed at how easy it is to hear the voice of the Lord and get His perspective when you follow His peace.

Day 7: The Next Generation

Quote of the Day: "To know the will of God, we need an open Bible and an open map" -*William Carey*

Verse of the Day: And David inquired of the Lord, saying, Shall I pursue this troop? Shall I overtake them? The Lord answered him, 'Pursue, for you shall surely overtake them and without fail recover all.' I Samuel 30:8

It was a new church that we had recently started on the edge of Bujumbura in a suburb called Kinama. Just down the road we had purchased land to help Pastor Jacques increase the size of the new congregation. He had a small home fellowship with about twenty people that met in someone's living room. A church in the US was coming out to erect a pre-fabricated metal tabernacle soon. The local believers would then be responsible to fill in the walls with mud and plaster. The congregation would quickly grow.

I had preached in Kinama a couple of times before without being overly impressed. The congregation had about 15 adults mostly in their 50s and 60s and about ten kids under the age of 10 that ran around like chickens with their heads cut off during most of the service. After multiple services like this in different locations I was beginning to dread being in Burundi. At times I had felt as though I had wasted my life by moving to this little nation. At times I wondered if God even know where I was?

At 27 years old my heart was tired of mostly preaching to older people with no desire to do much of anything with their lives. Where were the teenagers? The young adults? I wanted to see revival in the upcoming generation. I wanted to preach to the masses. My heart longed for God to send an awakening among the youth of this little nation. Some of this was selfishness; some of it just immaturity. Much of it was a genuine desire to see Jesus exalted.

Why did I have to preach again in another house church? I had decided years ago that I would go wherever God opened the door. In this season of my life most of the doors opening were in new congregations that felt dead. And truthfully, I was tired of it.

This particular Sunday morning as I prayed about the service I felt something stirring.

As is my normal practice I inquired of the Lord, *"What should I share? Please give me your heart for this congregation."*

The Lord directed my thoughts to Colossians chapter 1 verses 9-14. I decided to preach on the joy of knowing the will of God. I took off unpacking the idea: We will please the Lord. We walk worthy of Him. We will be fruitful in every good work. We increase in the knowledge of God. We are strengthened with His glorious power. We have patience and longsuffering. We give thanks to the Father for qualifying us to partake in the inheritance of the saints.

I suddenly felt as though this message was going to be for many young people. I asked the Lord to save at least seven. It seemed like quite a difficult thing to ask.

The day came. There were like 7 or 8 points that morning. I preached for at least an hour, but it was Burundi where services sometimes lasted three or four hours at one time so no one really objected to my 7-point message. Plus, the anointing of the Lord was really strong that morning. Communication flowed easily and effortlessly as I shared in Swahili. Pastor Jacques then translated into directly into Kirundi.

As I closed I gave an invitation to respond to receive Christ. The little house was packed from front to back with close to forty people. The smell of body odor was absolutely suffocating in the thick tropical heat. Several hands went up. I urged people to take the next step by coming forward—easier said than done as they literally tripped over one another. Seven young men, many kids, and several elderly adults stood before me. I felt the Lord's presence so strongly! God's Spirit had convicted them and their hearts were ready to receive.

Jesus had given me the desire of my heart. The funny thing is that I hadn't even noticed that they were in the audience due to the rather suffocating surroundings. I walked out of the little church there in Kinama that day mesmerized by the thought—God knew right where I was even when I felt discouraged.

Question of the Day: In what areas of your life do you need to experience victory? What can you do to allow Christ to work a complete work of freedom in these areas?

Musings: As I have grown in my walk with the Lord, I often find myself revisiting areas of former defeat. Rather amusingly, I find myself in similar situations, with similar people, and similar temptations. I often ask: *"Lord what am I doing here again?"* The answer is almost always the same: *"I brought you back here to reclaim everything that the enemy stole from you the first time around."*

Victory never tastes so sweet as when it is in an area where you were once humiliated and shamed by the forces of darkness. In such moments I find myself worshiping Jesus with renewed devotion—for I now have another crown of victory to throw at His feet!

I want to encourage you today. No matter how staggering the defeats of the past, God is in the restoration business. Relationships, finances, temptations, fears, doubts, etc… He wants to reign supreme in every area of your life!

You will probably have to go back to some past battlefields of shame and brokenness. Don't despise such moments for it is here that you will find a new God-confidence as you depend on Him to work victoriously in your life. It will require humility and brokenness, but in the end Christ will triumph. This will produce new joy inside of you as He shows you your true identity and calling. These lessons will in turn sustain you in battles yet to come. Trust me there is nothing like a win in an area of previous loss. Are you ready? Remember this is war.

Day 8: They Stole My Car

Quote of the Day: "Prayer is not overcoming God's reluctance, but laying hold of His willingness" -*Martin Luther.*

Verse of the Day: "Any branch in Me that does not bear fruit [that stops bearing fruit] He cuts away, trims off, takes away; and He cleanses and repeatedly prunes every branch that continues to bear fruit, to make it bear more and richer and more excellent fruit." John 15:2

       I was going to be speaking in Mustang, a little town outside of Oklahoma City. The venue was Saturday morning to a couple hundred young people. It was a Speed The Light Rally for those of you familiar with the program for mobilizing young people to give money towards missionary's vehicles. I had been asked to share for about 15 minutes on a Saturday morning.

In the weeks leading up to the Rally I had been feeling quite ill. I thought it best to travel down on Friday afternoon as there was no way I would make it on time if I tried to drive straight through on Saturday morning from my home in Tulsa. My good friend Eric is from Oklahoma City. He had been in a horrible car accident and needed a ride back to Oklahoma City. I asked if I could spend the night at his parents place if I took him down on Friday.

His parents welcomed the idea. We left Tulsa after dinner arriving around 10:00 PM. I unloaded my small backpack and went to bed almost immediately.

My alarm was set for 7:30 AM the next morning. I jumped out of bed, grabbed a quick bite to eat, got dressed, and brushed my teeth. I opened the front door of the house and headed for the car.

My 2004 Red Honda Accord had been parked in the driveway flush up against the garage door. A security light mounted on the awning of the house illuminated the entire street below. Eric's mom had been insistent. *"Park it there. That will be the safest place to leave it."* In the early morning cold it was nowhere to be seen.

My first thought? Eric and/or his parents were playing a practical joke. I headed back inside. *"So...did you move my car?"* I asked my friend still curled up in his bed.

"What are you talking about?"

"My car...is not there...did you move it?"

"Of course not."

The sickening realization dawned on me. It had been stolen. I called 911 immediately and within 30 minutes one of Oklahoma City's finest stood at the front door.

"What make was it?"

"2004 Honda Accord."

"You'll never see it again. We are averaging about 1000 Honda thefts a month in this part of the city. They are a hot re-sale vehicle."

A friend picked me up to take me to the rally. It was rather difficult to speak—a missionary gets his car stolen on the way to a missions rally to raise money for the purchase of other missionaries' cars. The irony of the situation was thick.

I borrowed a vehicle to get back to Tulsa. As I drove back I called Sach and narrated the story to him. *"Don't worry Steve. You'll have your car back within a week."*

"What? How can you be so sure?" I asked.

"We are going to pray and God will take care of it."

I found out later that he was on his first ever 40 day fast. Praying about a stolen Honda wasn't even a challenge compared to that kind of a spiritual undertaking. I watched in amazement as God answered seemingly impossible prayer requests that he laid before the Lord during that time of fasting and prayer.

Five days later, the Oklahoma City Police Department called me.

"We have recovered your car."

"Really? Where? How?" I couldn't believe it had happened so soon.

"There was a high speed chase before the suspects ran it into a street light. The front-end is in rough shape, but it's still drivable. We need you here within the next thirty minutes to pick it up."

"Wow! Wait, I'm in Tulsa. Can I send someone to pick it up?"

"Yes. We will wait."

I called Eric and he headed that way. Within fifteen minutes my vehicle had been recovered. Insurance paid for both the bodywork as well as the light internal damage; the two suspects were put behind bars. They were Mexican gang members who had randomly picked my car while cruising the neighborhood around midnight.

I called Sach with the news. *"They found the car and it has been recovered."*

"What else?"

"What do you mean?" I asked.

"I prayed for God to turn this into a blessing. God wants to do more."

A dear pastor friend of mine took up a special offering to offset the costs of a rental car as well as all incidentals. The check came in the mail a few days later. It was more than enough money to cover all my expenses.

I guess the gang members didn't count on one critical factor when they stole my Accord—the prayers and fasting of a former gang member 10,000 miles away crying out in **accord**-ance with God's will for my life.

Question of the Day: What might the Lord be trimming out of your life in this season? How are you responding to this process? What kind of attitude do you need in order to endure such seasons?

Musings: This story reminds me of the idea of pruning. I think pruning seasons are when God focuses on two main areas: identity and dependency. During harvest moments when fruit is bountiful the temptation exists to base one's sense of self-worth on results. In other words, when God allows us to be a part of the harvest we often get our ego strokes from the fruit blossoming around us. The problem with this tendency is that ever so subtly we start to move away from finding our sense of identity in being with Jesus to doing things for Jesus.

Is our ministry prospering? Are people coming to Christ? Is the business growing? It is easy to find identity in such exciting things. *"I'm a great soul winner, or I'm a gifted business person, etc..."* As our identity shifts from one of being to one of doing, another great danger arises. We begin to depend on our talents and giftings to continue the success we are enjoying. This is dangerous for the very reason that He alone must always be our sufficiency. The more success we experience the greater the potential to rely on ourselves instead of Him.

So how does God handle this scenario?

He gets out the pruning shears and begins to lop off some areas. Is this because He is angry and wishes to punish us? Hardly! John 15 is clear on this point. The purpose of pruning is never to punish; it's to force new growth and produce more fruit! We are forced to anchor our identity wholly in Him once again as we lean on our

Beloved in genuine dependency. Before long, our lives begin bearing more fruit! It's a beautiful process

Day 9: Baptizing 87 in the River

Quote of the Day: "God's work done in God's way will never lack God's supply" -*Hudson Taylor*

Verse of the Day: "Therefore put on God's complete armor, that you may be able to resist *and* stand your ground on the evil day of danger, and, having done all the crisis demands, to stand firmly in your place." Ephesians 6: 13

The invitation arrived from my dear friend Jerome Ndayisaba. He wanted me to accompany him on a scouting trip. I prayed and felt that this was God's will for my Saturday even though it involved quite a drive. I jumped into my Toyota Hilux pick-up paid for by the youth of Oklahoma and headed into the hills of Burundi.

We sped off down a bumpy road into the heart of Africa. Our destination was the little town of Nyabihanga situated in the literal middle of nowhere. After driving down a dirt track for about an hour we arrived at an outcropping of random buildings.

We found a rented mud building comprising two rooms—the roof was corrugated iron sheeting with tarps stretched taunt as an awning. The two rooms could accommodate about 40 people. As we pulled in, I was surprised to see over a hundred people sitting patiently on the ground awaiting our arrival. I assumed we had come to investigate the possibility of assisting with a new building project. Clearly, the church building was in trouble; by contrast, the congregation seemed alive.

It was a Saturday and I wasn't expecting anyone but the pastor and a few key leaders in the congregation to turn out. As we approached, they began to sing and dance. Pastor Daniel greeted us: *"Welcome! We are now ready to start the evangelistic meeting."*

I looked at Jerome, *"Evangelistic meeting?"*

"Missionary Steve we want you to preach."

"Preach?"

"Then we will have the baptismal service."

"Baptismal service?" I asked out loud.

"Then we will eat a meal together and go look at new properties for the church."

"New properties?"

Things had clearly evolved significantly—this was going to be an all day event and maybe then some. Praise and worship started. People danced and sang with great enthusiasm under the tarps. News had spread throughout the area of our arrival. People started coming from everywhere. I knew that I would soon need to preach the word.

I felt the Lord whisper to my heart, "*Speak on the Second Coming.*"

It would be the first time in my life I had preached on the Second Coming. I launched into the Word God had placed in my heart from I Thessalonians chapter 4. I spoke in Swahili; Jerome translated into Kirundi. The message was very short, lasting less than 25 minutes.

It was so cool to see God work. I had never really spoken much in a mass evangelism context. This was my first time. It was so amazing to feel the Spirit of God sweep through the crowd. As we closed in prayer and gave the invitation, Pastor Jerome made it clear, "*We are going to baptize those of you who are responding.*"

Less than five minutes later we were headed towards the nearby river. Hundreds stood on the riverbanks to watch as Jerome and I divided those desiring to be baptized. He took half and I took half. We stood in the frigid mountain stream up to our waists. After a prayer of instruction, people waded into the river one after the other.

"Muri zina ya Data. Muri muzina ya Mwana. Muri zina ya Mpwemu." In the name of the Father, the Son and the Holy Spirit.

Down they went one after the other. For at least 45 minutes it continued unabated. Jerome handled one side of the river as I baptized the other side. After all was said and done 87 people had made a public declaration of their faith in Christ. I have no idea how many were already members of the church and how many had responded in the evangelistic meeting.

All I know is that it was awesome: one of the most rewarding afternoons of my entire life. I felt so energized—doing God's will that Saturday had fired me up. We changed clothes in the bushes underneath a little tarp and headed back into Nyabigina to look for pieces of land for the church.

We never found anything. To my knowledge no missionary ever went back. It wasn't too much after this that I had to leave the country. I never saw Pastor Daniel again and I think that the church is still meeting in the two little rooms. Someday I want to go back and facilitate the construction of a permanent structure.

Obviously, God's will that day wasn't to build a church; it was to build the Church!

Question of the Day: What is God's will for your life? Does this thought scare you or excite you? How do you search out God's will for you?

Musings: *"What is the will of God for my life?"* Have you ever asked that question? From an early age I constantly thought about it. Growing up the enemy tried everything possible to convince me that the will of God for my life was something heavy, difficult, dull, and dreadful.

Have you ever felt that way? Once I started doubting God's intentions towards me the enemy would capitalize on my insecurity. He threw every lie in the book my way—trying to get me off track with God's purpose for my life.

Thank God I never explored these options very far simply because Holy Spirit was so faithful to show me the lies and the danger awaiting me on the other side of them. They were nothing but a scam to steal and destroy my God given purpose. One day the light came on for me as I was reading Romans 12:2. *"Do not be conformed to the pattern of this world, but be transformed by the renewing of your mind."*

Sounds good, but why do I need to have my mind renewed? The answer hit me between the eyes, *"then you will be able to discern what is the **good**, **pleasing**, and **acceptable** will of the Lord."* Since that moment I have never doubted that His intentions and plans for my life are for my good! His will, when accepted with a renewed heart and mind, is pleasing and acceptable! God has good things in store for you. Don't fall for the enemy's scams and lies. Let your heart, mind, and spirit be renewed in His Word and Presence and soon you will be able to see clearly again.

Day 10: I've Brought My Answer

Quote of the Day: "If a commission by an earthly king is considered a honor, how can a commission by a Heavenly King be considered a sacrifice?" -*David Livingstone*

Verse of the Day: "When you pass through the waters, I will be with you, and through the rivers, they will not overwhelm you. When you walk through the fire, you will not be burned *or* scorched, nor will the flame kindle upon you." Isaiah 43:2

Over the course of about 3 months I built a relationship with Joeli. He is a young Tanzanian who works as a night guard at the house where I lived in Dar Es Salaam. He was a very quiet, pensive sort of fellow, who never usually talked except to ask for his salary.

Several years ago he represented Tanzania in the East African Power Lifting championship in Nairobi. It's the only time he had ever been out of the country. As you can imagine, he's a pretty defined guy. I would almost go so far as to say that he's as strong as me, but it's good to remain modest about things like this.

What amazed me about him wasn't so much his muscle definition, but rather his physical strength. His capacity to lift things was remarkable. I remember seeing him grab a stack of chairs some ten or twelve high, lift them above his head, and hoist them on the top of my Land Cruiser as though it required no effort at all.

He grew up Catholic, but hadn't attended church in years. And had no intentions of changing. We had several conversations about God since I was serving as the pastor at the Ocean International Community Church and often had people visiting the house. He wanted to know why I was such a popular person. Each time the conversation shifted towards heavenly things I came away thinking that he was totally disinterested. At about the three month mark of our interactions he one day asked me for a Bible. I was surprised, but quickly procured a Swahili version. He read it on and off for several weeks.

One night when he had nothing better to do than watch a steel gate on the front of the property and I had nothing better to do than try to avoid being bitten by Tanzanian mosquitoes, we talked in greater depth.

"If you left work today where would you go?" I asked.

"Oh that's simple," he responded. *"I would head home."*

We chatted about his home for several minutes-
the area of town he lives in, the part of the
country he comes from etc...

"*What if you were to leave this life today Joeli,
where would you go?*" I continued.

"*Err...I don't know...*" he replied somewhat
intrigued. "*I think that's a very important
question*" he continued.

As we talked I felt to challenge him: "*Jesus can
give you assurance in your heart that you will go
to heaven to be with him...are you ready to take
that step?*"

"*Hmmm....no, not yet,*" came his pretty decisive
response. "*Give me one week to think about it
and I will come back to you with my answer next
weekend when I'm back on duty*".

I assumed he was putting me off so I smiled
graciously and remarked that I should probably
get back into the house before the mosquitoes
had sucked all my "mzungu" blood.

One week later the rains came very heavy,
indeed. For hours and hours it just poured. No
one came to the gate to see me and I didn't get
outside to go talk to Joeli during the rain. When I
finally emerged I had missed him—he had
already gone home.

About a week later we met again when he was on duty. We chatted about the rain and the need for more. He didn't seem too talkative as I tried my best to be pleasant.

He suddenly stopped me half way through my sentence: "*I came with my answer Steve but you weren't around.*" The look in his eyes told me that he was hurt, deeply hurt.

"*Your answer?*" I thought to myself. "*Surely, you don't mean what we talked about last week?*" I continued to process.

I cut my thought process short so that I could properly apologize. "*Pole sana Joeli,*" I offered in Swahili.

He continued: "*I still have the same answer today though.*"

Really? I could see the hunger in his eyes. "*My answer,*" said the former Tanzanian power-lifter "*is that I want to give my life to Jesus.*"

We prayed together in the driveway. Jesus touched him as He always does anyone anywhere who comes with such a heart-felt answer.

He was facing many daunting challenges on several different levels that kept him from being able to trust the Lord. There financial pressures at home, physical challenges with his wife, and ongoing tension between them. The rivers, fires, and waters of Isaiah forty three seemed all around him. Yet, he had decided that it was better to walk through these situations with Jesus holding his hand rather than trying to do so without Him.

Question of the Day: What situation are you facing in your life that seems overwhelming right now? How have you been approaching it? What would change in your attitude if you were sure that Jesus was right there in your life?

Musings: I have faced my fair share of difficult situations over the years. One day, while I was reading Isaiah 43:1-2 the word *when* leaped off the page at me. The thought came so strongly: "It's not a question of *if;* it's a question of *when*."

In other words, we will all face rivers, waters, and fires in this life. No one is given special exemption. Some people live in denial trying to confess away their problems—this has never made much sense to me. Why pretend something isn't happening when it really is? This doesn't demonstrate faith; this demonstrates an inability to process reality. And worse, it short-circuits Jesus's desire to reveal Himself to us in such challenging moments of life.

Our world isn't looking for fake people who have no issues in their lives. Rather, they are looking for real people who have learned to soar above the storm by trusting in Jesus. Only when we go through something can we truly speak to hurting people with His kindness and authority. Someone once said that a testimony always begins with a test. Could the storm in your life really be an opportunity for spiritual growth and increased ministry opportunity?

Being able to minister to people has nothing to do with fancy theological words, titles, and positions. Instead, ministry has everything to do with sharing His compassion and mercy in the face of human brokenness. Where do we learn this? Rivers, waters, and fires. Never fear—He has promised to walk with us. Remember His name will always be *Emmanuel*—God is with us.

Day 11: Hemorrhoids for the Road

Quote of the Day: "Anywhere, provided it be forward—farther still farther into the night" - *David Livingstone*

Verse of the Day: Search me thoroughly, O God, and know my heart! Try me and know my thoughts. And see if there is any wicked *or* hurtful way in me, and lead me in the way everlasting. Psalm 139:23-24

During my first year of living in Madagascar I made a most painful discovery one day—hemorrhoids. I was 32 years old at the time. The discovery was difficult for me to process. I was very active, running several times a week. I ate a very healthy diet. How could I have suddenly developed hemorrhoids? It just didn't make any sense to me at all.

I began to pray about the matter asking the Lord to heal me as the state of the roads in Madagascar ensured that my condition wasn't going anywhere anytime soon. Bailey and I were engaged at the time—she in the United States and me in Madagascar. We used to talk via Skype twice a day. Often the connection was terrible.

"Hello? Can you hear me?" started most conversations and usually found its way into the

rest of the conversation a couple of hundred times. Okay, I'm probably exaggerating, but you get the point.

No single guy in their early thirties wants to share with his fiancée that he is dealing with hemorrhoids. I remember the day I mustered the courage to tell her.

"Bailey, I need to tell you something. I'm ummm....well....dealing with hemorrhoids."

Long pause in the line.

"Hello Bailey? Can you hear me?"

More long pause in the line.

"What did you say?"

"I said....ummm....there's hemorrhoids."

There was giggling followed by, *"Sorry, but it sounded like you said you have hemorrhoids."*

"Yes, that's exactly what I said."

More giggling.

Bailey promised to do some research and see what she could find out for me.

A few days later the General Superintendent of the Madagascar Assemblies of God called me on the phone to remind me that I had promised to drive to Fianaratsoa with him to speak at a pastors conference.

I didn't have the courage to tell him about the hemorrhoids so I searched for another option.

"Could you take a bus?" I asked in my politest possible French.

"No, of course not. We must go together."

"Could you take your car?"

"No, I promised the pastors that you would be there."

Perfect. Fianaratsoa is only a mere 9 hours south of Antanarivo where I lived on some of the windiest pothole filled roads that I have ever seen. It is quite a daunting drive under normal conditions. Hemorrhoids? Well, it wouldn't be pretty. I continued to pray.

The next time Bailey and I spoke she told me about a remedy online—papaya and salt water.

The next day I went to the market and bought the biggest papaya you have ever seen. I promise. It was gi-normous! I ate papaya until my belly hurt. Within a few hours it was gone.

No change. So I bought another one and devoured it. No change. I remember the saline solution and so I decided to take a salt bath.

No change.

More salt water. More papaya. No change. I even tried eating papaya while in the salt water.

This went on for days. No change.

The phone rang the day before our scheduled departure. It was pastor Oeli, the General Superintendent. *"Can we will leave tomorrow morning as we planned?"*

I just didn't have the heart to say no. *"What time?"* I asked.

"5 AM."

Early the next morning we departed for Fianaratsoa. Pastor Oeli asked me to drive, as he wasn't feeling too great. The irony was thick in the vehicle.

It was quite a sight to behold. I balanced myself on one cheek making sure to take the pressure off a certain spot. Pastor Oeli only looked at me oddly a couple of times due to the strange body posture I adopted to survive the arduous trek.

Three hours into the journey the car stalled on the road. We had to find people to push the car. Let's just say I wasn't much help on that one.

We were able to get a mechanic to take a look. He got the vehicle running again.

"Whatever you do, don't let the car stall out again."

"Umm…we are headed to Fianaratsoa," I responded.

"Don't let it stall out again."

We finally made it Fianaratsoa. It was excruciatingly painful. In the first service, pastor Oeli asked me to come up to the platform and preach. I wasn't prepared and the assembled pastors gave me a strange look as I hobbled around the platform like a very disgraceful ballet dancer.

At the close of the message I felt the Lord drop something very clear into my heart, *"There's someone here with a bleeding issue that I want to heal."*

"You have to be kidding me God."

The inner battle raged fast and furious. I argued with the internal prompting. I tried to explain it away. In the end though, I decided to obey sharing what was in my heart and asking the individual to raise their hand.

No one responded. I felt very foolish.

I closed the service in prayer and retreated to the privacy of my Chinese hotel (this is a story in and of itself). To say I was angry would be an understatement. I wrestled with the Lord in prayer. There was no answer.

Early the next morning we returned to the venue as a rather large lady stood behind the pulpit and shared in Malagasy as tears poured down her face. I grabbed a translator.

"What is she saying?" I demanded.

"She was in the room behind the platform yesterday when you were speaking. She has been lying in bed for several months with a bleeding issue. She raised her hand when you asked for a response, but no one could see her."

I froze mesmerized by what I was hearing. I felt the conviction of the Lord. He was dealing with my heart and teaching me a very important lesson.

"You're so impatient Stephen Kuert" I thought to myself.

"During the night the power of God touched her and she immediately sat up completely and totally healed."

The tears pouring down her face now started to trickle down mine. It was so moving. A few moments later God broke loose in that service. Heaven came down. Pastors were weeping and praying with intensity as Jesus touched His people. It was one of the best pastor's meetings I've been in.

The next morning when I woke up I realized that something glorious had happened to me too. Yep, you guessed it. My hemorrhoids had totally disappeared. God's timing is so wonderful. His touch is so powerful. His conviction is so beautiful.

Question of the Day: How do you respond when Holy Spirit convicts you? What kind of response do you think the Lord is looking for?

Musings: Conviction. This word goes hand and in hand with another word: sensitivity. In order to feel the pains of conviction there must be a corresponding measure of sensitivity to the Lord. I know many who boast: *"Oh seeing such images* *or hearing such words doesn't bother me anymore."*

I can't tell you how many times I have heard this recently. Anymore? When we ignore conviction something must give. And that something is the sensitivity of our hearts to His voice. We are no longer bothered by something *not* because we have reached a new level of maturity, but rather because we have reached a new level of compromise and hardening. What is true of sins of commission is also true of sins of omission.

We often pride ourselves that we haven't done anything wicked or overtly evil. Maybe we haven't fallen for a particular sin in a while. Of course, this is valuable. Yet, we must go much deeper than this in our walk with Jesus. He is not after people who don't do anything bad. He's after people that work righteousness on the face of the earth. People who respond to His voice. People who advance the Kingdom not just talk about the Kingdom. We are called to do the good works He has prepared for us (Eph. 2:10).

Atherosclerosis is defined as the hardening of the arteries in and around the heart muscle. This condition is certainly nothing to brag about. Each passing day in this state is one day closer to an untimely demise. Likewise, each moment resisting His conviction only hardens our hearts more against His voice and His gentle love. The key idea here is His voice. If you would know the voice of God intimately you must practice prompt obedience when He deals with you, whether in the area of commission or omission. Remember He loves you and wants the best in your life. Responding to His voice increases our capacity to hear Him with greater clarity.

Day 12: A Supernatural Run

Quote of the Day: We have eternity to tell of the victories won for Christ, but we have only a few hours before sunset to win them. -*Anonymous*

Verse of the Day: In conclusion, be strong in the Lord [be empowered through your union with Him]; draw your strength from Him [that strength which His boundless might provides]. Put on God's whole armor [the armor of a heavy-armed soldier which God supplies], that you may be able successfully to stand up against [all] the strategies *and* the deceits of the devil. Ephesians 6:10-11

I remember going for a run on the beach just south of Mombasa, Kenya several years ago. I had been crying out to God for the supernatural in my private prayer times. As often happens in this part of Kenya, a young man tried to sell me marijuana as I stretched out.

"*Do you want some good stuff?*" he asked in broken English.

Coastal Kenya gets lots of tourists who abuse drugs. So the local "beach-boys" try to make money by coercing people into buying their goods—often cocaine or marijuana. I didn't want to be bothered so I told him that I already had the good stuff.

"*Where did you get it?*" he asked, rather concerned that someone else had stolen potential business. I don't remember my exact answer, but it was something to the effect: "*Jesus gave it to me.*" I started running.

The young man called out after me, "*Jesus? He gave you the good stuff?*" Confusion filled his voice.

"*Yes,*" I hollered back over my shoulder.

Returning from my thirty-minute jog, I was surprised to see the young man sitting in the sand waiting for me.

He asked me if I was serious about receiving the good stuff from Jesus. I witnessed to him in Swahili for a few minutes. He told me that he was a Muslim and didn't believe much of what I had to say. His eyes, though, told a different story. They were full of hunger for God's love.

After we finished our conversation he asked if he could introduce me to his uncle. "*No problem,*" I responded. The next afternoon we again met up on the beach. He led me down a sandy trail heading towards a small village. In an isolated spot a man was waiting for us. He introduced me to his uncle. I wasn't very polite because I was worried about getting mugged.

The uncle asked me if what I had told the nephew about Jesus was true. "*Oh yes!*" came my candid response.

"*Jesus has the good stuff?*"

"*Yes,*" I felt the need to explain my position so I started to share.

"*Jesus is the Son of God?*" he asked inquisitively.

"*Yes!*" I replied again.

The uncle then rolled up his trousers to expose one of the most hideously infected wounds I've ever seen. He had been in a terrible accident some weeks previous and the wound was festering. "*Is your Jesus able to heal me right now?*"

I was speechless. No one taught me how to handle the whole Muslim needs healing on the beach scenario when I was preparing for ministry. I quietly stammered in the affirmative quite unsure of what to do next. I decided to kneel in the sand and place my hands on this man's shoulders as I offered a simple prayer asking for a demonstration of the power of God.

Moments later God's presence fell very heavily.

All three of us began to cry. I had the privilege of leading both men to Jesus. The uncle's leg was miraculously healed. And I left the beach with a newfound conviction: the supernatural is for today!

As a side note, the last time I saw these men, several years after this story took place, they were both still living for the Lord and had introduced their families to Jesus. They attend a Pentecostal church in Ukunda. God's power radically transforms lives!

Question of the Day: In what area(s) of your life do you need supernatural intervention? Have you asked Him? Why or why not?

Musings: God expects us to be obedient to His voice, move forward with His revealed will for our lives, and implement the truth of His Word in our areas of influence. Sometimes in this process of walking out the practical day-to-day steps of our faith, impossibility will stand in our way daring us to keep advancing. It could be a financial mountain, a physical issue, a relational crisis, false accusations, spiritual attack, or some other overwhelming obstacle. They are never easy, but don't lose heart.

How do you handle such moments? For me the key is found in Ephesians 6 in one simple word: "Stand". How long do you stand? Until He intervenes on your behalf so that you can keep moving forward. What if you lack the strength to stand? Verse 10 of this chapter tells us to be strong in the Lord and His mighty power. This is so important in order to gain victory in a spiritual battle.

How do you take such a stand? We must be clothed with His mighty armor and the offensive weapon of His sword. Why is it so difficult to stand? This is spiritual warfare; you aren't wrestling against flesh and blood. What do you do while you are standing? Pray with all manner of requests and petitions. Why do you need to stand? There are valuable Kingdom relationships, influence, and territory connected with your stand.

Several years ago I pastored a church in Tanzania. Things weren't going too well at all. Finances were short. Services were dead. The congregation had no vision and volunteers were virtually nonexistent. It was really rough going, but I knew God had placed me there. Instead of quitting, I decided to stand. In desperation, I called two members of the church to pray with me. For several months we sought God together twice a week.

One day in December, the heavens opened during our prayer time and God gave us a breakthrough: the entire atmosphere of the church changed, people started coming to Christ, finances boomed, and unity prevailed. We had stood our ground and God intervened!

Practically speaking this means that we need to do all that we can do and then wait in expectation for Him to do what only He can do. This is the supernatural intervention part. And trust me it makes all the standing and waiting worth it!

Day 13: Jesus, The Money Changer

Quote of the Day: "Love is the root of missions; sacrifice is the fruit of missions" - *Roderick Davis*

Verse of the Day: Looking away from all that will distract to Jesus, Who is the Leader *and* the Source of our faith giving the first incentive for our belief and is also its Finisher bringing it to maturity and perfection. Hebrews 12:2

Living in Burundi required constant finances. Money in. Money out. We continually needed Burundian Francs which are known as Frambu for short. The exchange rate fluctuated all the time. And when exchanging large amounts of money a differential of even 5 Frambu per dollar made a big difference. There was one sure person to contact to get the best rate in town—Jesus. He was the best moneychanger in town.

Actually his name is Isa which is Jesus in Arabic. (It's my story though and I want to use his English name. If you tell it you can use Issa.) A Burundian entrepreneur, Jesus, had started his own Forex business years before our missionary team showed up on the scene. When we did show up on the scene though, he gave us preferential customer treatment. At least five Frambu higher per dollar than on any other offer in town. We had his cell phone number and would call him up prior to an exchange. "*How much can you give us today Jesus?*"

He would always answer by saying: "*How much are you bringing?*" And so the negotiations would start.

When we had to purchase large pieces of land he would be especially thrilled. I remember one specific occasion. We were buying a piece of land in the heart of downtown Gitega to plant a new church with Pastor Jerome Ndayisaba, the current General Superintendent of the Burundian Assemblies of God.

I know, I know, for most people it's not exactly a thriving metropolis, but for Burundi it is big stuff. The second largest city in the country no less. And the price of land costs a pretty penny, or maybe I should say a pretty Frambu, comparatively speaking of course. Donors from the US wired the money to the mission's account.

I withdrew US dollars in Kenya and made the call to Jesus.

"*How much can you give us today Jesus?*"

Same old reply. "*How much are you brining?*"

I coughed nervously before answering. I didn't like the idea of telling anyone how much money I would be brining with me. After all, this was Burundi, one of the poorest and most violent nations in the world.

"*How much*???" Jesus responded rather shocked.

"*In that case I'm going to give you the best rate you've ever received.*"

Off I went to downtown Buja to find Jesus at his favorite spot, the Forex Bureau. I brought two duffle bags and a backpack with me to carry out all the money I was about to receive. As I walked in, the guy behind the counter greeted me: "*Hey Steve how are you?*" before yelling over his shoulder: "*Jesus, Steve is here.*"

"*Send him back.*"

The iron gate opened that protected the inner sanctum of the Forex Bureau where all the money was stored. I heard the clank of the key locking the bolt in place behind me as I headed straight towards Jesus' office. After the usual pleasantries, I produced the cash all in brand new $100 dollar bills. Some of Uncle Sam's very finest now belonged to Jesus and his little Forex business. Jesus went to the safe and opened it up. Out came the Frambu. Stacks and stacks of it. I filled my backpack. Then I filled a duffle bag.

And half of another one. It was a lot of money. Sixty-five million Frambu if I remember correctly. I felt rather sheepish carrying so much money. For the first time in my life I was a real bona-fide millionaire.

As I walked out, Jesus asked if I needed help carrying the bags out. *"Nope, I should be fine. I parked outside on the street."*

In hindsight I realize how stupid this answer must have sounded. I walked into a Forex Bureau in one of the most crime-ridden cities in the world with 3 empty bags only to reemerge a half hour later with all of them stuffed to the hilt.

Nevertheless, I made it home safely, drove to Gitega a few days later, made the transaction, purchased the land, hosted a construction team, built a tabernacle, finished the walls, and started a church that runs several hundred to this day with 8 church plants, all because of a man named Jesus—both, literally and spiritually.

I think of our conversations fondly. *"How much can you give me today Jesus?"* And I wonder if that's not how many of us approach the real Jesus. *"What's in it for me today Jesus?"*

Or to be more crass, *"If I serve you today what will you give me?"* And while I think there is more to it than the simple answer that Jesus the

Burundian gave me, I like to think that it's a really good starting point, "*How much are you brining*?" He asks in return. In other, words how much are you willing to surrender?

Question of the Day: What is your Kingdom assignment in this season of your life? How are you focusing your attention and energy into accomplishing it? Where have you been sidetracked? How can you get back on track?

Musings: One of the greatest challenges in life is staying focused. Just ask the pilot who misread his instrument and landed in the ocean! Focus has everything to do with accomplishing our Kingdom assignment. What engages our time and attention? Where are our resources going? What voices are influencing our decisions and perceptions? All of these questions relate to focus.

Personally, I find that everything falls into place in my life when I keep an eternal perspective alive: my giving, my time management, my relationships, my decisions, and especially my attitude. When I was in college I read the story about Jonathan Edwards, a great preacher in the 18th century. He used to pray: "*Oh God stamp eternity on my eyeballs.*"

In his pockets he kept two little precious stones to remind him that his work would one day be judged by fire. He wanted to receive an eternal reward for his labors. I realized how intentional we must be with our own hearts and minds if we want to live with eternity burning inside.

How do I do this? I listen to music about heaven. I meditate on the promises in the Word about the rewards for the faithful and the overcomers. I study passages on the judgment of believers. I ask for eternal perspective when I pray and seek the Lord. I spend time with people who have a like heart. I read books about this topic: John Bevere's book Driven by Eternity is a good one.

I invest my life in others—time, finances, encouragement, and discipleship. I share my faith with people who don't know Christ. I set aside days for prayer and fasting to renew my passion for the Lord. All of these things help maintain the right perspective.

Remember that you and you alone are responsible before God to accomplish His eternal purpose for you. This is best accomplished when we live in the light of eternity!

Day 14: Holy Spirit Bar Encounters

Quote of the Day: "Without prayer, even though there may be increased interest in missions, more work for them, better success in organization and greater finances, the real growth of the spiritual life and of the love of Christ in the people may be very small" -*Andrew Murray*

Verse of the Day: But you shall receive power (ability, efficiency, and might) when the Holy Spirit has come upon you, and you shall be My witnesses in Jerusalem and all Judea and Samaria and to the ends (the very bounds) of the earth. Acts 1:8

After Sach first gave his life to the Lord I knew that there was going to be some great challenges for him moving forward. He lived with his girlfriend at the time, drank heavily, and surrounded himself with some very unscrupulous 'friends'. I would often possess such a heavy burden to pray for him. It was clear that he was a man of great influence. The enemy would want nothing more than to pull him back into his old lifestyle.

While praying one day I felt the gentle nudge of the Lord in my heart, "*You need to share about the Holy Spirit with Sach and his friends.*"

We had been meeting every Friday afternoon in the local *Sheraton* bar to share the Word and pray. A side room served as our small group hangout space. Believe me the name is about as far away from *Sheraton* standards as anyone could possibly get. There were no furnishings; we provided our own seats. Nevertheless, the small group had grown to about 15—this number mostly consisted of former drunkards, drug addicts, criminals, and prostitutes.

I prepared a simple message on the power of the Holy Spirit in the life of a believer based on passages in Acts 2, Acts 10, and Acts 15. I talked about a distinct and subsequent experience from salvation available to all believers that would empower them to live a life of greater witness and consecration to Jesus.

There were blank stares in the little *Sheraton* bar room that Friday afternoon. I might as easily have talked about speculative future commodities or ancient Near-Eastern literature motifs. I could tell no one had ever heard anything about this before; they were finding it hard to believe. *"Invite them to receive my Spirit's power."*

Thus, began the internal dialogue between my rational side and the voice of the Lord.

"You can't be serious Lord."

"Invite them."

"They already think I'm a raving lunatic for sharing this stuff."

"This is the moment."

I stopped, took a deep breath and slowly, but methodically gave the invitation.

"Would any of you like to receive the fullness of the Spirit's power in your life?"

Sach looked at me rather confused. *"Do you mean right here in the bar? I thought that was reserved for the four walls of a church building?"*

"Umm...Holy Spirit can meet us wherever and whenever we are hungry to encounter His presence."

"Okay, then. You can pray for me," he volunteered.

I felt compelled to add one more thing, *"When you receive the fullness of Holy Spirit don't be surprised if you start praying in tongues."*

"Tongues?" The whole room looked at me like I was out to lunch.

"You know....Heavenly languages that Jesus gives us...." Nobody had any idea what I was talking about. *"Never mind...let's just pray."*

The small group looked at me. I started praying and placed my hand on Sach. Most of the others just watched. I asked the Lord to come with power and fill Sach. Nothing happened. I prayed some more. Still nothing happened. I opened my eyes and could see the look of disbelief etched on many faces as if to say, *"See we told you so...this is craziness."*

I felt rather sheepish and very awkward. I could see my little car parked outside the bar through the little window. I wanted nothing more than to get out of that bar and never come back. I felt like a total fool.

"Let's close in prayer and we'll meet back next week," I stated knowing full well that I had no intention of ever leading another meeting in that room again.

"Lord we thank you for your word today and that we have had the opportunity to meet together."

As soon as we said, *"Amen"* I was going to make a beeline to the vehicle.

I finished praying. Suddenly, there was a loud noise form the other side of the room where Sach had been sitting. I looked up perplexed. He was kneeling on the ground next to a wooden bench shaking like a leaf.

Several looked at me in disbelief as if to ask, *"What did you just do?"*

Within moments the atmosphere changed in the room. God's presence was heavy and real like an unseen wave crashing against human hearts. Some went to their knees; others wept, still others laughed. A couple of the young men cried out for forgiveness. The Holy Spirit had come in a tangible way.

Question of the Day: Have you experienced the power of the Holy Spirit in your life? What kind of difference has it made? How has it changed you?

Musings: I know there is a lot of confusion over this idea of being filled with the Holy Spirit. I experienced much uncertainty about it growing up. I knew it was real; I just didn't know if it could be real in my life. For many people it is kind of a badge or trophy that you use to measure a past spiritual experience that sadly, has almost no influence on their day-to-day life.

When I received the power of the Holy Spirit in college my life changed in a very significant way. It wasn't immediate, but it was progressive.

And it had everything to do with the presence of fear in my life.

Growing up I had a great problem with anxiety and worry. This continued well into my early 20s. This created personal spiritual tension. I believed Christ paid for my sins and had a plan for my life in a general sense, but experienced precious little faith in my heart for anything else. I feared almost everything: the enemy, physical ailments, lack, the future, death, plans for my life, etc...

I believed the worst about myself. I accepted all kinds of lies about my identity and calling. I was intimidated. I walked in rejection convinced people didn't like me. There was a cloud of fear over my head—unsure as to whether God was for me or against me. My prayer life amounted to nothing more than that of a spiritual beggar making lots of requests and plenty of noise, but seeing precious few answers and very little of His presence in my life.

This affected my self-perception terribly.

I was the most miserable of Christians you have ever met. No joy. No life. Constant fear. Anxiety. Worry. Doubt. It was horrible. Thank God this all began to change when I experienced the power of the Holy Spirit in my life on a continual daily relationship. II Timothy 1:7 became a great blessing in my life.

"For God did not give us a spirit of timidity (of cowardice, of craven and cringing and fawning fear), but He has given us a Spirit of power and of love and of calm *and* well-balanced mind *and* discipline *and* self-control."

God's Spirit is a Spirit of power and love. He is a Spirit of calm and a well-balanced mind. He produces self-control and discipline. As Holy Spirit became a personal friend He broke the shackle of fear.

This transformed the way I saw the Bible. It was no longer a collection of words about God; rather it was the literal words of God to me. Soon I found promises that released hope inside of me, lifted my spiritual vision out of the garbage heap to the glories of heaven, produced life inside my spirit, stirred me to believe for great things, and dared impossibilities for Him. I no longer only believed in God. I now believed God. What a huge difference it has made every since.

Remember this: you are called to live everyday with the same faith that you exercised when you received Christ as your Savior. The Holy Spirit's power makes this not only possible, but enjoyable!

Day 15: Helicopter Rainforest Missions

Quote of the Day: "Those who reject the authority of God's Word quickly lose any impetus for evangelism and missions" -*Jerry Rankin*

Verse of the Day: "For His divine power has bestowed upon us all things that [are requisite and suited] to life and godliness, through the [full, personal] knowledge of Him Who called us by *and* to His own glory and excellence (virtue). By means of these He has bestowed on us His precious and exceedingly great promises, so that through them you may escape [by flight] from the moral decay (rottenness and corruption) that is in the world because of covetousness (lust and greed), and become sharers (partakers) of the divine nature" 2 Peter 1:3-4

One of the coolest things I've ever had the privilege of doing as a missionary is flying by helicopter into remote villages deep in the interior of Madagascar. I've been privileged to travel with my friend Doctor Aaron Santymire on several such visits. We usually take several other people along to make the visit as profitable as possible. Flying fast and furious over the rainforest is an incredible experience.

Landing in the middle of villages that don't have electricity, running water, or any kind of basic health services is unlike anything else I've been around. Let me try and describe it:

The dust whips everywhere off the ground as the helicopter slowly settles down into a grassy field. People come running from all directions mesmerized by the sight and sound of a helicopter. Within moments of touching down there is usually a crowd of several hundred assembled in the tropical rain forest. Palm trees are everywhere. Little mud huts dot the cleared areas of forest.

We quickly set up a portable sound system to introduce ourselves as a medical team present to treat any physical ailment in the village. As people begin to line up for consultation we share the Gospel message and give an opportunity to respond. For the next several hours we will treat scores of people before jumping in the helicopter to fly to the next village in the rainforest and repeat the process over again. We try to coordinate the visit with a local church plant to give the pastor in the village exposure and merit.

Sound fun? It's incredible.

One particular afternoon we landed in the middle of a larger village. The lush green surroundings were breathtaking. Within moments there were hundreds gathered. A local Malagasy pastor

announced our intentions over the sound system.
The next thing I know I hear my name.

"Missionary Steve will preach."

"Preach?"

I had no idea that I was to preach. We had talked
about sharing a word of greeting, but no one had
said anything about preaching. I was present as
an observer and medical facilitator.

I'm very much a visual person so I fished around
inside the helicopter and found the holsters for
the helicopter props to hold them in place during
a strong wind. I grabbed these and decided to
start at the very beginning—Genesis. I search for
a member of our team to be Jesus—Paul Balela,
my dear friend from Tanzania. Then, I searched
for someone else to be Satan—Alihasiana, one of
my dearest Malagasy friends. I narrated the story
as they did their best improvisation acting.

God creates man in perfection. Satan hates God
so he lashes out at Adam and Eve with treachery
and deceit. Sin enters the picture. Humanity
becomes enslaved. At this point I wrap my arms
with the helicopter holsters. They are so long that
there is still 10 some feet of rope on either side of
my arms. I give one end to Balela…I mean Jesus
and the other end I hand to Alihasiana aka the

devil. The tug of war for the destiny of humanity ensues.

Then satan gets the idea: why not just kill Jesus? Meanwhile several hundred Malagasy watch the impromptu illustrated message taking shape in the middle of the rainforest. The cross comes into the picture. It seems as if hell's diabolical scheme has triumphed. Then unbelievably Jesus rises from the dead. Sin is vanquished. Death defeated. Disease conquered.

The heat is sweltering as the intense jungle humidity engulfs everyone present. Yet, another factor has also come into play: the anointing. It's no longer just an impromptu Gospel message. The gravity of the situation sinks in—precious Malagasys are hearing the Message for the first time, ever. Souls are hanging in the balance.

Balela, I mean Jesus, rips the holsters off my hands. Freedom! Forgiveness! Relationship with God! My translator and dear brother in Christ, Henintsoa keeps up in the local Antaimoro dialect. We give the altar call together as nearly everyone present raises their hands to surrender their lives to Christ. It's glorious! God is clearly doing something powerful in this remote corner of Madagascar.

Pastor André leads the crowd in prayer sharing the details of the new church being planted in the little village. We pray for people and then attend to their physical needs for several hours. Soon we will pack it all up and fly to the next village where Paul Balela and Pastor André are planting another church and do the same thing. Over the course of a week we will visit eight some sites, all in previously completely unreached villages in the Eastern coast of Madagascar. It's amazing to see God at work!

Question of the Day: Do you read what you believe? Or do you believe what you read? What influences your decisions? The Word of God? Or your personal experiences?

Musings: The Word of God is absolutely vital to experiencing a vibrant relationship with Christ. Today, I want to give you a little challenge. Identify areas in your life where you are continually battling the enemy—this could be temptations, fears, doubts, etc… For example, let's take the lie of rejection.

Now do some study in the Word. Find specific promises that deal with your situation. Returning to our example, let's take Ephesians 1:6 from the King James Version: "*He hath accepted us in the Beloved.*" Memorize this promise from the Word of God. Begin to meditate on it throughout the day by quoting it to yourself whenever you remember. Once this promise moves from your head to your heart and you begin to believe it things will start shift in your life. Don't believe me?Try it.

This is exactly how I overcame rejection—a shackle that paralyzed me for ten years. Every time the thoughts and emotions associated with rejection tried to govern my thought process and perception of myself I would quote Ephesians 1:6. One day after quoting this verse hundreds if not thousands of times—the truth of it hit home. Heaven opened in my dorm-room at college and Jesus delivered me from this lie concocted by hell itself. There is nothing so powerful as faith combined with the promises of the Living God!

Now let's apply this to missions. God's Word commands us to go. His love compels us to share. His Spirit empowers us to make His Word and His love real to those around us.

For me this is Ephesians 6:19. I've been praying it over myself for twelve years now. "Pray also for me, that freedom of utterance may be given me, that I may open my mouth to proclaim **boldly** the mystery of the good news, the Gospel." This verse has given me courage on more than one occasion to preach with boldness.

Day 16: Hidden Treasure

Quote of the Day: Christ wants not nibblers of the possible, but grabbers of the impossible. " — *C.T. Studd*

Verse of the Day: Teach me Your way, O Lord, that I may walk *and* live in Your truth; direct *and* unite my heart [solely, reverently] to fear *and* honor Your name. Psalm 86:11

It was one of those things that I felt I had to do before I left Burundi. There was a little wildlife reserve just outside of Bujumbura, the capital city. When I say little I mean little. You could easily walk across this piece of land in 20 to 25 minutes. It had once boasted quite an array of wildlife species: all different kinds of antelopes, primates, birds, hippos, crocs, as well as other plains animals such as zebra. I was there to find treasure of the animal variety.

Rumor had it that the world's largest crocodile once lived there. From the only video footage ever captured of the legendary Gustav by a Belgian herpetologist, Patrice Faye, this monster croc is said to be between 25 and 30 feet long. Throughout the city of Bujumbura people say that he has eaten hundreds of people and even taken direct flank machine gun fire as he skirts the banks of Lake Tanganyika.

Is it just urban legend? Hard to say. I once met Patrice Faye high in the mountains of Burundi in a pygmy village. I think he was as surprised to see me as I was him. We were distributing clothes and sharing the message of the cross in a pygmy village. I'm not quite sure what he was doing, but he was convinced that Gustav was a very real crocodile, very much alive, at least as of 2008. After watching the video of this massive croc, I wanted to see him. I expressed my desire to see the giant reptile to some friends.

They suggested I visit Gatumba Nature Reserve the last place he had been seen. So just months before I moved out of Burundi I jumped into my vehicle and drove to the front gate. It was no more than a twenty minute drive from where I used to live. There I found the entrance fee quite reasonable because hardly anyone visited the park anymore.

Most of the animals had been wiped out during the war. People needed food and anything that moved was served on the menu. It was still standard policy that a guide accompanies the car, not so much for the African wildlife as for the human wildlife hiding with guns in the bushes.

Having grown up in Kenya, where the animal varieties are endless, I was reluctant to have a guide. Especially a drunk one who reeked of the local brew, but rules are rules, and maybe this was the right man to help me find Gustav.

We started the drive down the sandy trail. Ironically enough, my guide's name was Stephen. I found out that he was a Congolese refugee who had been living in Burundi for several years to escape the pillaging rebels in his home area. He lived in Gatumba the little town on the Congolese Burundian border.

We talked about Congo, his family, and why he had turned to the local brew. He was hurting deeply from wounds of the past, poverty of the present, and hopelessness for the future. He saw no way out. As he shared his sob story I suddenly remembered my mission for the day: Find Gustav. Remembering my real quest I shared my desire to see the legendary monster.

He laughed. The croc hadn't been seen in years and he speculated he either had died from old age or was on a circuit around the longest lake in the world and might reappear in the future.

Disheartened, I asked what other animals there might be to see. His prognosis wasn't too optimistic. There were egrets and hippos. I laughed to myself. In Kenya, we had egrets in our backyard and hippos in almost every river and lake in the country. Not to mention that just a few months earlier a hippo had interrupted our volleyball game right there on a beach in Bujumbura (another story for another day).

I turned the vehicle around to exit the park. Nearing the gate, I felt as though I had wasted a day chasing after imaginary crocodiles in the heart of Central Africa. Then it happened, very slowly, but surely. My heart became aware of a greater purpose in my visit. My steps had been orchestrated of the Lord, not to find a crocodile but a prodigal.

I asked my new friend if he knew anything of Christ and His great love. He had heard the message years before, but it had never really made much sense. I shared about my own battles with hopelessness and feeling bound by sin until Jesus intervened.

Just moments later heaven came near and Stephen began to cry. We prayed together. Before parting company I told him about a little church we had just planted in Gatumba pastored by my dear friend from Congo Doctor Gerard Cizungu. He promised to check it out.

A couple of weeks later I called Cizungu. We talked about several different matters.

"*A strange thing happened recently missionary.*"

"*What was that Cizungu?*" I asked politely.

"A man that we have been praying for the past several months came to church this past Sunday and said that he met a muzungu (white man) who told him about Jesus."

"What do you mean you had been praying for him?" I asked rather surprised.

"His wife comes to church here and we have been praying for him to find Christ."

My heart leapt inside of me. I had been searching for a hidden treasure: Gustav. Heaven had been searching for a different treasure: Stephen the animal guide who had a handful of faithful believers praying for him.

Question of the Day: Is there a besetting sin in your life that you haven't been able to overcome? How has it affected your relationship with the Lord?

Musings: I had fallen into the same sin yet again. I kept promising the Lord that I wouldn't do it. I had fasted, I had prayed, I had wept, I had sought godly counsel, and I had memorized scripture—over and over again. Yet, I kept returning to the same place. Why couldn't I overcome this area?

As I meditated on the issue, I finally realized that part of me, somewhere deep down inside just didn't want to let to go. Most of me wanted to live for Jesus and keep His word, but there was still a dissident movement lurking beneath the surface. I had a divided heart.

I had no clue, though, on how to move forward. I felt like a hypocrite even though I loved the Lord and desired to serve Him. As I read Psalm 86:11 the light bulb went on. For the first time in my life I saw the connection between a whole heart and the fear of the Lord. The fear of the Lord is the reverential honor and respect of God's holiness that makes us hate anything that would keep us from Him.

Only when we reverence a Holy God and fear being separated from His glorious presence more than we love our sinful secrets can we experience freedom. I saw David's cry in a new light. He is praying for a whole heart so that he can experience the fear of the Lord.

I have become convinced that the most important element in our personal relationship with Christ after salvation and the power of the Holy Spirit is the fear of the Lord. Exodus 20:20 tells us not be afraid as the Lord places His fear on our lives. Sound contradictory? The verse continues by saying that His fear enables us *not* to sin. Did you know it's possible to live free from sin? Jesus didn't save us to leave us enslaved in bondage. He saved us for glorious freedom. He saved us to triumph over compromise. He saved us to overcome and know the sweetness of victory.

I will never forget the day the Lord broke the power of the sin that had controlled me for so many years. He placed His fear on my life and since that day by God's grace I haven't gone back! He gave me a whole heart so I could fear Him. And His fear keeps my heart whole. I would invite you to do a study on the fear of the Lord. It is one of the most wonderfully enriching Word studies in Scripture. Check out the many references in Proverbs and Psalms that list the promises connected to it.

Yes, you can be free! Yes, you can know victory. And yes, once you are free there is a whole new dimension of authority and intimacy waiting for you.

Day 17: The British Counsel and Wilberforce

Quote of the Day: "Live simply so that others can simply live" -*Dwain Jones*

Verse of the Day: "And He who is seated on the throne said, See! I make all things new. Also He said 'Record this, for these sayings are faithful (accurate, incorruptible, and trustworthy) and true." Revelation 21:5 Amplified

I was invited to attend a farewell dinner party for an outgoing staff member of the US Embassy in Burundi. Diplomats thronged the luxurious setting of the outdoor deck overlooking Bujumbura. Most of those present occupied prestigious positions for their respective governments here in the nation of Burundi.

I had interacted with most of the people sitting around the table at least once. Nevertheless, I only really felt comfortable around one of the British guys. We had played volleyball together several times over the course of a year or so. I wouldn't say that we were friends as much as good acquaintances. His name is P. and he was also a part of the football team I joined in Bujumbura. We used to play twice a week in the evenings at a local athletic club called *Entente Sportive.* The floodlights had serious electrical issues often meaning the field would go completely dark in the middle of a game. Swarms of mosquitoes would follow us around the field as our bodies dripped sweat in the intense humidity. I digress, however, from the story at hand.

For several weeks I had been reading *Amazing Grace* by Eric Metaxas. It is the incredible story of William Wilberforce and his epic battle against the evil of slavery. The book impacted me deeply. To this day, I still think it ranks among the top three books that I have ever read. The chapter on his conversion moved me to prayer. At the age of 21 Wilberforce was elected to Parliament as a popular political figure. A friend, Isaac Milner, shared Christ with him while on a European tour. He had been raised in a godly family, but turned his back.

God convicted the young man's heart and nothing would be the same. The famous songwriter John Newton encouraged the young politician to use his political platform to reform British society.

A series of events had been set into motion: slavery would eventually be abolished because of one man's tenacity to pursue justice and righteousness. Behind the scenes had been a radical conversion. This book left an indelible mark on my heart to pray for God to save a new generation of Wilberforces.

All these thoughts were still very fresh in my mind as I sat down next to my British friend for dinner. I could tell that he was present at the farewell dinner in an official capacity.

I knew P. worked for the British government, but I didn't really know what he did in Burundi. We started to talk. He soon explained that the United Kingdom didn't have an official diplomatic mission in the nation of Burundi due to the political tension in the Burundian government. However, they did run a Liaison office in Bujumbura to facilitate relations between the two nations.

P. was the coordinator. He explained his job responsibilities in more detail: security detail, political analysis, U.K. representation, democratic lobbyist, negotiation, etc… It was pretty extensive. He regularly interacted with all the top political players in the country: the president's office, the official rebel groups, the US government, East African leaders, South African leaders, ambassadors, etc… Not bad for a young man in his mid-twenties.

"Have you ever heard of a guy by the name of William Wilberforce?" I asked certain that he would respond in the affirmative. Surely, this would generate some good conversation.

"Whose that?" he asked somewhat distracted.

I thought that he must not have heard me correctly.

"You know, William Wilberforce, the great British orator and politician who abolished slavery."

There was a total blank expression on his face. *"I've never heard that name before."*

I continued rather unsure of myself now. I shared the details of the story I had been reading just sure that something I was saying would jar his memory. After all, the abolition of slavery is no small political feat and here was an intelligent member of the British government.

From time to time, P. would interject, *"That's brilliant, what an amazing story"* into the conversation. He has a huge heart for the downtrodden and under-dog so it was easy for him to identify with Wilberforce and his passion to see slavery eradicated. Around us other diplomats discussed political scenarios, economic factors, human rights abuses, and local currency shortfalls. All the while, our conversation intensified around the life of a British politician now dead for 180 years.

As we talked I became aware of the Holy Spirit's presence. This was a divinely orchestrated conversation. I leaned closer to P. and gently said, "*I believe that you are a William Wilberforce of this generation.*" To this day I believe it was one of the most anointed and yet simplest of prophetic words that I have ever shared with anyone. Paul could feel the weight of it as much as I could. We talked for a while longer before parting ways that evening.

Over the course of the next few months we became good friends watching FA Premier football matches, playing volleyball and football, eating pizza, and talking life and politics.

We both left Burundi about the same time to head our separate ways. I moved to Tanzania and he headed to Afghanistan. In the past 5 years we have seen each other twice: once in Tanzania when he flew to visit me in Dar. He stayed for about five days. One night he participated in a home group meeting where we prayed and studied the Word of God. God's presence was there strongly. As he left for the airport the next morning, with tears in his eyes, he stated that his heart had been moved during that time together.

"*Whatever you do Steve, don't stop sharing this God stuff with others,*" he finally mustered.

I guess it was my turn to receive a prophetic word. As far as I know he has not yet made a personal decision for Christ.

The other time we connected was in New York City at the United Nations where he got Bailey and I into the temporary General Assembly hall. We took some pictures and talked about life before I felt prompted to remind him of God's purposes on his life. He smiled and thanked me as sincere and genuine as ever. I know the Lord is working and I still believe God to accomplish this word in his life

Question of the Day: What areas of your life need to be made new by the Lord? Are there places in your heart and mind that need to be renewed by His grace?

Musings: I love what David prayed in Psalms 51. *"Create in me a clean heart, O God, and renew a right, persevering, and steadfast spirit within me."* The Hebrew word for create in this verse is *barah*. It is the same word that appears in Genesis 1:1. It means to create something new out of nothing. In other words, David is crying out for something that doesn't exist—a pure heart in the midst of his ugly sin and brokenness.

Remember that this man, David, is one after God's own heart. He is considered one of the greatest worship leaders to ever sing songs of praise to the Lord. He has triumphed over towering giants. And been entrusted with the solemn task of restoring the ark to Jerusalem. He is not some pagan; this is one of God's most trusted servants. No wonder God sends the prophet Nathan to expose the hideous skeletons hanging in the closet of his heart. God nails him.

Before we pick up stones to condemn David for his hypocrisy and the stench rotting in the recesses of his heart and mind, let's be honest. We all have such skeletons hidden away in the secret places of our hearts and minds. Yours may not be murder, adultery, seduction, and deception, although it could very well be. Yours may be something far more benign in your personal estimation. The issue here is not the classification of the skeleton, but its effect—on you, on those around you, and on your relationship with the Lord.

I know people who have allowed small offenses from the past to become mountains of bitterness literally eating them alive from the inside out. For others it might be gluttony? Or anxiety? Pride? Fear? Enough said.

David knows his sin is egregious and wicked. Yet, instead of hiding it or trying to pull a fast one by covering it up, he does the unthinkable. He brings it into the light recognizing that only the miraculous intervention of the Lord can transform his heart. So he cries out in brokenness: *"Barah!"* *"Make it new!"* *"Put something in me that isn't there!"* It's bold. It's desperate. It's faith.

I think this is where the prophetic comes into play. When we understand the will of God and combine it with faith we are releasing a prophetic statement concerning God's purpose for the future. Prophecy produces newness in people's hearts and lives to believe God for heaven's destiny to be released.

God intervenes and in a moment works in that unseen place where body, spirit, and soul are all interconnected. David walks away from the encounter different—he's new on the inside. And this newness brings wholeness to his life.

I see this as being one of the most critical matters in a person's life. Why? Whole people are used of God to heal people. Hurting people hurt people. Which are you? From personal experience I can tell you that God makes even the most ugly of wounds whole. He wants to make us new.

Day 18: His Prayers Give me a Headache

Quote of the Day: If a commission by an earthly king is considered an honor, how can a commission by a Heavenly King be considered a sacrifice?- *David Livingstone*

Verse of the Day: Do not be conformed to this world, this age, fashioned after and adapted to its external, superficial customs, but be transformed (changed) by the entire renewal of your mind by its new ideals and its new attitude, so that you may prove for yourselves what is the good and acceptable and perfect will of God, *even* the thing which is good and acceptable and perfect in His sight for you. Romans 12:2

One day Sach invited me to come speak at a secondary school in the Kahawa area, just outside of Nairobi. It was where he had gone to high school prior to dropping out prior to graduation due to financial issues. He still had several administrative contacts in the school that had heard that he had given his life to the Lord.

Intrigued, they wanted him to come and share his story. There was a Christian club that met after school and Sach thought that it would be a really good opportunity if I came along to speak after he shared his testimony. We went with several of his other friends—some believers, some not. We arrived as classes were closing for the day. One of the main teachers asked Sach to pop his head into a couple of the classrooms and announce what he would be talking about in the Christian club just a few minutes later.

In normal Sach fashion he had entire classrooms laughing in a couple of minutes as he shared a brief overview of his story. I stayed outside talking with the other guys that came with us. One was a Southern Sudanese refugee named Riak. At the time several hundred of these dark slender Dinka people lived in the neighborhood where I had first met Sach. He was close to six foot eight, slender as a rail, and had a dream of immigrating to Canada.

He was considered the coolest kid in his college preparatory school—something of the Kenyan version of a junior college. We had played basketball a couple of times and he had some crazy skills. He liked Sach and didn't mind hanging out with me as long as it involved basketball and buying him lunch, which I usually did. When things turned towards Jesus, however, he checked out quickly. There seemed to be some kind of invisible spiritual resistance holding him back.

The teacher responsible for the religious club invited us into a nearby classroom as school closed for the day. Sach headed our way with a stream of young people following. Soon the room was filled to capacity as some stood against the back wall. Sach shared his testimony of encountering Jesus out of a lifestyle of alcohol and crime as a matatu tout (the guy who hangs out the side of the door to collect money from passengers). Many of the students recognized him as he had serviced that particular area of Nairobifor several years. This created almost instant rapport.

Sach finished and introduced his "mzungu" friend. I opened to Isaiah 59:5 and shared a message entitled "Snake Eggs and Spider Webs." The message focused on the spiritual battle for our minds. About ten minutes into the message I realized that the entire room had come under conviction. I don't think I've ever felt such ease in preaching as I did in that public Kenyan high school. I poured out my heart as Jesus ministered to these precious teenagers.

In closing I invited Sach to give the altar call. Hands shot up everywhere, even teachers wanted to receive Christ. About the only person who didn't raise his hand was Riak. He sat with his arms folded staring at me, clearly not amused.

Sach didn't miss a beat. After leading people in a sinner's prayer he called people to come forward that needed special prayer.

"Steve will now pray for you," he stated.

"Umm...okay," I thought to myself. I certainly hadn't expected such a response and young people poured to the front. I started to lead out in prayer.

"Steve, you need to lay hands on people," Sach instructed.

I invited to Sach to join me. The head teacher also came forward to pray with people. Riak stood up afraid of being singled out. Everyone assumed that he was already a believer. I could tell he was getting really uncomfortable; he didn't want to attract any attention his way.

As we prayed the Lord worked in a great way. Many students wept. Some needed further prayer for salvation. Others wanted prayer about family situations. Some had addictions. Riak stood stiff as a board against the blackboard staring in disbelief as people were touched all around him. As I walked from student to student I walked right past him and felt that I should pray for him.

"Can I pray for you too?" I asked quietly.

He looked like a frightened little schoolboy even though he towered head and shoulders above everyone in the room except Sach.

He nodded. I felt the Lord's presence descend, but also a sudden cold sensation. It was very bizarre. The more I prayed the more rigid he became—straight and stiff with his shoulders held high. I felt as though this was an unseen spiritual battle and continued praying. Riak started to scoot away from me and backed all the way back up against the blackboard. There was nowhere else to go—he was flanked by students on either side, the wall behind him, and me in front of him. More praying. He grabbed his head in his hands as though trying to block his ears. He looked absolutely miserable.

I stopped praying. "*Riak,*" I whispered, "*Jesus loves you.*"

He still held his head in his hands. Finally, he whispered back, "*Your prayers give me such a headache.*"

"*My prayers?*" I asked unsure of what to say.

"*Yes, my head hurts so bad and I feel cold all over.*"

"*Would you like to receive Christ like we've talked about?*"

"*No.*"

I stopped praying for Riak. He slowly relaxed and stopped holding his head. We closed out the meeting. Many had responded; it was a great victory. My heart was saddened though about Riak. We talked many more times, but he never showed much interest in Jesus. Several months later he was granted amnesty by the Canadian government and flew to Alberta where he became a disc jokey. I haven't seen him since.

I often wonder about the dynamics of spiritual warfare. I'm not sure what the coldness or the headache was about—although I have my suspicions. It is very interesting that the message had to do with the mind and he kept holding his head in hands while praying. I believe 2 Corinthians 4:4 offers a key, *"The god of this age has blinded the minds of unbelievers."*

Question of the Day: How is the Word of God changing the way that you think? Is the way that you think indicative of the way that you act?

Musings: I was reading my great-grandfather's Bible one day. He was a great man of God at the turn of the 20th century primarily serving as a pastor in Canada. In his more than one hundred year old Bible he had written clearly in the margin: *"Sow a thought, reap an action; sow an act, reap a habit; sow a habit, reap a character; sow a character, reap a destiny."*

The words leaped off the page at me. I knew that this was a serious scriptural principle that carried great weight. Clearly, my great-grandfather thought it was important enough to write in the margin of his Bible. Thoughts ultimately control destiny. There is such power in our thinking. To this day I see my thought life as being one of the most important indicators of how I'm doing in every other area of my life. There is so much that could be said about this subject.

I once preached a message in Dar entitled, "What I say when I preach to myself." I got the idea from a message I heard Jentzen Franklin preach years ago. The idea is basically that we have internal self-talk going on all day every day. What we think about really determines the kind of messages that we send internally. One of my favorite preachers is Reinhard Bohnke.

I love the guy. His accent and preaching style make me smile. When I used to get really discouraged in Burundi I would stand in front of the mirror and try to imitate Reinhard Bohnke. In my best German accent I would holler, *"God is going to make a way for you Stephen Kuert. He has great plans for your life. You are a History Maker and World Changer."* Something would lift off me. The point is that there is something so powerful about the way we think and speak.

Let's focus on the verse of the day. The way we think about ourselves and about God is of utmost importance to our life. Romans 12:2 makes it clear that when the Word of God doesn't renew our minds we aren't able to find God's perfect will for our lives. Transformation of our minds comes by the Word. Yet, the Word doesn't just jump off the pages of the Bible and tackle us. It has to be memorized, meditated, spoken, claimed, quoted, etc… in order for it to really begin to work in our lives. Yes, we need an ongoing experience with the Word of God.

Day 19: The Energizer Bunny Taxi Ride

Quote of the Day: "No reserves. No retreats. No regrets." -*William Borden*

Verse of the Day: So he got up and came to his [own] father. But while he was still a long way off, his father saw him and was moved with pity and tenderness [for him]; and he ran and embraced him and kissed him fervently. Luke 15:20

I had been on the little island of Mafia for a couple of days doing ministry with a team of high school students from the U.S. Several weeks prior to my visit one of my best friends, Kevin Schneider, asked me to connect with a team of university students from Oral Roberts University back in Dar Es Salaam, Tanzania where I was living at the time.

I exchanged communication with the team and the only time they had available was an afternoon prior to their return departure to the US. It would be tight, but I could make it work with my schedule. Landing at Julius Nyerere International Airport in Dar Es Salaam I jumped into a taxi and asked the driver to take me to the hotel where the team was staying.

"*It's on the other side of the city,*" he responded.

"*Just get me there,*" I smiled.

"It will cost more."

"No problem."

We crossed to the other side of Dar on the ferry and an hour after touchdown I entered the hotel asking the taxi driver to wait on me.

It was a divine appointment—the first time I have met Bobby Parks, the current director of ORU missions. We have been friends ever since. We talked for several hours, before saying good-bye. The team would shortly be headed to the airport; I needed to get back to my house on the other side of town. It was a Sunday so I hoped that traffic wouldn't be too heavy.

We zoomed away back towards the ferry that would carry us towards downtown Dar-Es-Salaam. As we reached the ferry, the taxi driver began sharing part of his life story.

He had been raised up country near the Moshi area. For several years he worked odd jobs in and around this part of the country. There he landed a job as a truck driver that soon took him all over East and Southern Africa.

It was blazing hot. The AC in the taxi didn't work. I was going on minimal sleep. My newfound friend had no intentions of slowing the narration so I just nodded my head in agreement.

"*Sawa sawa,,* " I would say every so often to indicate that I was listening, but not really all that interested. I wanted to take a nap.

He wasn't deterred in the slightest. More details. More events. More of his life story. He kept pouring on the information.

We reached the other side of the channel only to find that the roads had been closed due to the recent return of the president. Whenever he landed at the airport much of Dar would be shut down to give his caravan exclusive access to the roads. We sat for two hours hardly moving at all. I was soaked in perspiration. The sun blazed into the little Toyota Corolla taxi. The driver had scarcely taken a breath in between his stories.

"*Then I went to Zambia with the company. It's a very interesting country Zambia—there are lots of open markets with every sort of vegetable.*"

"*Sawa sawa.*"

I secretly prayed for the roads to open up so I could get back to my place and get some peace and quiet.

The taxi driver continued unhindered by my disinterest. He was on to why life had become boring on the open road and how he had decided to return to Dar-Es-Salaam as a taxi driver. This had been a pretty good decision as the money wasn't bad and his wife was happy to have him closer to home.

"I wanted a more stable life and to stop having to travel all the time."

"Sawa sawa." This guy had more energy that the Energizer Bunny.

Traffic had just started to inch forward again. The accumulation of vehicles would guarantee bumper-to-bumper traffic the whole way home. This was the taxi ride that just wouldn't end. We had already been together 3 hours and I had hardly gotten in a word.

"You know many years ago a team came to my village to hold special meetings. During these outdoor meetings they prayed for sick people and preached the Gospel. One of the blind people in the village was healed."

For the first time in hours the guy had my attention.

"The message was very touching. The American visitors preached about being born-again. My entire family responded for salvation that day."

"What about you?" I was amazed that the conversation had taken such an unexpected turn.

"No, not me. I'm an alcoholic and a very broken man. I missed my opportunity."

I couldn't believe my ears. Could this be a divine appointment? The sweat poured down my face as I began to share about the Prodigal Son and a Father in heaven who gives the second, third, and thousandth opportunity to respond to His grace.

"Sawa sawa," it was his turn to respond as I shared.

The words poured forth from my heart. I suddenly had new strength and new clarity. I felt such a sweetness of His presence. I knew that only Jesus could turn a never-ending taxi ride into something of eternal value.

We pulled into the driveway at my house. It was well past 7 p.m. We had been on the road for hours.

"Would you like to give your life to Christ?" I asked as I fished in my pocket to find enough money to pay for the marathon trek.

The divine appointment that had been lingering for thirty plus years finally became a reality as my new friend knelt in the driveway to ask Jesus into his heart and to forgive him for wasted time. It was such a sweet moment as we swatted mosquitoes while calling on the name of the Lord. I'm forever grateful that Jesus didn't let me miss out on what He was doing that day.

Question of the Day: Are you making yourself available to be used of the Lord? How can you position yourself to cooperate with His purposes?

Musings: While in university a group of my friends traveled to Houston, Texas for spring break. Two of the guys were from Houston and came from the same church. We stayed with their parents. The pastor of the church came over one day to talk to us. We were planning on starting a missions organization to send other university students into some of the difficult places of the world like Aghanistan, Iraq, etc...

Pastor Dave spent several hours with us talking about different aspects of ministry, integrity, and walking with the Spirit. It was really good stuff. We broke for lunch and I had the opportunity to ride with Pastor Dave in his car. I wanted him to continue sharing his thoughts. One of the things he said on that car ride has impacted me for over a decade now. He said that when it comes to ministry he stopped trying to make things happen for God. Rather, our responsibility as Christ followers is to ask two simple questions: *"Father what are you doing in this situation?"* Secondly, *"How can I be a part of what you are doing?"* I have chewed on these two ideas for years. They have marked the way I see ministry.

My responsibility isn't to try and make something happen. That's intense pressure; neither can I sit back and adopt a laissez-faire approach, that's apathy. Instead, I must seek to position myself to hear what the Spirit is saying and seek to implement it accordingly.

I, sincerely, believe that this was Jesus' approach to ministry as well. He often made astounding statements like, "By myself I can do nothing..." (John 5:30). Surely, as God's Son there was plenty that He could do. Yet, He is demonstrating a ministry model of partnership and intimacy with the Father. Jesus spoke what Father said. He did what Father was doing. Nothing more, nothing less.

This posture requires humility and dependence on the Spirit to reveal this intimate model of living out our lives. He wants us to work with Him—not for Him, and certainly not without Him. I think the temptation in ministry is to try and call the shots. We come up with the plan and the agenda and then ask God as a by-the-way to bless what we are doing.

I believe we are living in an hour where Luke 15 is going to be fulfilled. The prodigals are going to start returning to the Father. Divine appointments and destinies that have been left hanging for years and maybe even decades are going to intersect with broken lives. We must model Christ's example of ministry in order to share the Father's heart for reconciliation.

Day 20: Militia on the Runway

Quote of the Day: "I never prayed sincerely and earnestly for anything but it came at some time; no matter at how distant a day, somehow, in some shape, probably the least I would have devised, it came" - *Adoniram Judson*

Verse of the Day: "Most assuredly, I say to you, he who believes in Me, the works that I do he will do also; and greater *works* than these he will do, because I go to My Father. And whatever you ask in My name, that I will do, that the Father may be glorified in the Son. If you ask anything in My name, I will do *it.* John 14:12-14

Our helicopter had been parked overnight at the Manakara airport. It was a small mold ridden building a few hundred feet from Madagascar's Eastern coastline. It had once been fully operational with direct flights to Antanarivo a couple of times a week for French tourists desiring to get a little R&R. Economic sanctions coupled with political instability changed this drastically. The airport saw only a few chartered flights a year now.

When we had landed the day before, a well-dressed man had come running out of the airport to see the strange sight of several white people disembarking from the iron bird. His tone and attitude were both hostile as well as combative.

"Who gave you permission to land here?"

The pilot of the helicopter was a former French military Special Forces who had seen action in some hairy corners of the world. He had already regaled us with stories of the Kosovo War back in 1999. As such he didn't take kindly to the cold reception.

"We filed papers in Antanarivo. They called ahead to tell the airport that we were coming." He retorted.

"I wasn't alerted of your coming. They never called."

"I was in the air traffic control office when they called," he shot back.

Since he had no official uniform, badge, or identification of any kind we brushed past him to meet our contacts waiting for us on the ground.

We had planned an evangelism, fact-finding, medical trip to several small villages in the surrounding forested areas of Manakara. The plan was to spend the night in Manakara so we could pick up three additional passengers for the mission. It would require two trips to each village as the helicopter could handle 5 people including the pilot and we now had a team of 8 people.

Since the villages were so close to Manakara it wouldn't be difficult to use the airport as a central hub to ferry people back and forth throughout the following couple of days.

Early the next morning we all assembled at the airport. There wasn't a person to be seen anywhere except an elderly watchman whose sole responsibility in life was to clear the runway for the few flights that visited Manakara. He used a whistle to chase people and sometimes goats off the landing strip. It was pretty funny to watch, but I digress.

As the helicopter warmed up and the first part of our group was whisked away to the interiors of Madagascar's rain forest, I noticed this man on his cell phone. He seemed rather excited in his communication.

A few minutes later the helicopter roared back into sight and myself, my friend Aaron, and a Malagasy medical doctor known as Dr. Fils jumped on board the waiting chopper. Our pilot had to find a restroom before taking off and went into the airport building for a few minutes. As we waited the chopper blades screamed above us in full rotation. Suddenly, I noticed a several jeeps speeding down the airport road.

It looked like military personnel. As they neared, the turret of a mounted M-60 became evident. Several heavily armed Malagasy soldiers jumped off the back of one of the jeeps. All weapons were pointed in our direction as the helicopter pilot emerged from his potty break. It looked like big trouble.

Aaron and Dr. Fils jumped off the helicopter and headed in that direction. I could see soldiers yelling as gun barrels pointed directly at my team members. The gentleman from the day before emerged from one of the jeeps now clothed in full military regalia. The insignia on his uniform indicated he was a colonel in the Malagasy army.

"You are spies!" He yelled.

"We are not spies." Our French pilot yelled back.

"You have no clearance to be here and you are under arrest."

"We filed paper work yesterday!"

"That's not true. I'm impounding the helicopter and taking you all to jail."

It was a heated argument to say the least. I started praying at the top of my lungs in the Spirit. The helicopter rotors screamed so loud that no one could hear me, except hopefully the Lord.

Our pilot reached into his pocket. *"I'm going to call the General of the Malagasy Armed Forces."*

The colonel scoffed in total disbelief.

Both men were at tipping point. The tension was so thick that I feared what would happen if he was bluffing.

Ring. Ring. Ring.

I prayed more fervently hoping that this wasn't some paramilitary stall tactic. I yearned for the General to actually pick up.

No response.

"I told you that you are under arrest." The colonel lost no time in capitalizing on the change in momentum to take advantage in the argument.

I sighed. This wouldn't be pretty.

The cell phone started to ring.

"Yes? Hello? General? Yes, this is Jean Christophe. We are in Manakara and we need your help. I'm talking to one of your men that is out of order in full violation of Malagasy domestic air travel code."
"He wants to talk to you." The pilot smugly handed the phone to the colonel.

I couldn't believe this was happening.

"Yes? Sir? What?"

The phone hung up. Within moments all weapons were withdrawn and official apologies were issuing forth. We were promised full protection while in the area and that no one would be allowed so much as to get within a kilometer of the helicopter while it was parked on the runway.

"You really know the General that well?" I later asked my new friend.

"Oh yes. This kind of stuff happens all the time here in Madagascar and he gave me his personal cell phone number in case there is ever any trouble."

I was impressed to say the least.

"How do you know him?" I asked one final question.

"We go to church together."

Question of the Day: What does prayer look like to you? How do you see your interactions with God in this area?

Musings: Besides missions and spiritual awakening, prayer is probably my favorite subject to talk about. I think the three go together. If we pray we will have spiritual awakening and develop a heart for missions. If we are connected to missions we recognize the need for spiritual awakening and so cry out in prayer. These three pursuits are essential for the work of God to go forward with any kind of effectiveness in our generation.

Prayer is a deep subject that many authors have written on very extensively. My thought on prayer for today is that we must have awareness that we are not wasting our time. In other words, prayer is a productive endeavor.

This is basically what faith entails in this area. We believe that God wants to hear us. We believe that He has the power and authority to do something about what we are asking. And we believe that He will release His power and authority on our behalf, both in us and around us. Without these three convictions prayer becomes a meaningless religious activity.

Truthfully, I think this is part of the reason why so many Christians have so little time to seek Jesus. They simply don't believe that there are any results from their praying. We could talk about motivation, perseverance, holiness, etc… as factors of prayer. At the end of the day though the bedrock condition for prayer is faith—a confidence that when we get on the phone to the General of the Armies of Heaven and Earth there will be a response. It may not be immediate, but at the right time there will be a corresponding intervention from heaven as a result of our prayers.

Day 21: Authority in the Forest

Quote of the Day: "In order for the existence of such a ministry in the Church, there is requisite an authority received from God, and consequently power and knowledge imparted from God for the exercise of such ministry; and where a man possesses these, although the bishop has not laid hands upon him according to his traditions, God has Himself appointed him" -*John Wycliffe*

Verse of the Day: Jesus approached and, breaking the silence, said to them, All authority (all power of rule) in heaven and on earth has been given to Me. Go then and make disciples of all the nations, baptizing them into the name of the Father and of the Son and of the Holy Spirit, Teaching them to observe everything that I have commanded you, and behold, I am with you all the days perpetually, uniformly, and on every occasion, to the close *and* consummation of the age. Matthew 28:18-20

We landed in the middle of the forest somewhere north of Antanarivo in the middle of the thickest jungle that I have ever seen. I jumped out of the helicopter grateful to be on solid ground again. Our approach through the mountain canyons had left us quite wobbly.

People began running from everywhere to gather around the visitors emerging from the steel bird. As we set up the medical distribution stations and the hand-held speaker, people stared in amazement at the visitors from the sky. Clearly, no one in this village had ever seen a *"vahaza" (foreigner)* before.

The Malagasy pastor with us, Pastor Zaka, addressed the crowd explaining our intentions as well as how the medical team would function. I wasn't paying too close of attention when I heard my name.

Great. Here we go again. I began to share as Pastor Zaka translated. People listened quietly as I made some introductory remarks.

As I began to preach about the cross of Christ something interesting happened around us. There was an almost immediate sense of disturbance that swept through the crowd. I've never seen anything quite like it before. Several little kids got into a fight screaming bloody murder at one another. I said something else about Jesus and immediately a new distraction unfolded—a couple of drunk ladies began squabbling in some huts on the perimeter of the crowd. They were just close enough to cause everyone to turn their heads in that direction.

I continued to preach hoping that I could regain people's attention. Quite to contrary, things got much worse. Suddenly, a pack of wild dogs burst out of the forest and ran right into the middle of the assembled crowd. They were barking and baying as though they had treed some poor animal. People began shouting and throwing stones to try and drive the dogs away. Almost simultaneously, several younger men began to go to blows. Even if all of the commotion hadn't been taking place I felt as though my words were falling on the ground in front of me.

Sheer pandemonium continued in and around the helicopter. I stopped preaching and handed Pastor Zaka the microphone. *"Please continue for me,"* I whispered. He could tell that I was deeply frustrated. Zaka took the microphone to try his hand at the preaching.

I knelt on the ground next to Zaka feeling such a holy anger inside of me. I could tell this was intense spiritual resistance, but I had no idea how to handle it. I began to pray quietly to myself. *"This resistance needs to be rebuked,"* I mused internally.

"Yet, how can I accomplish this when pandemonium rules the day?" I continued to ponder. *"I don't have the microphone in my hands anymore and even if I did and could pray out loud would that change things?"*

I was sort of praying/asking questions at the same time.

Like a flash of lighting a thought leapt up in my spirit. *"Authority has nothing to do with volume."*

Quietly, I prayed over what I sensed in my heart. True authority is based on surrender to the Lordship of Jesus Christ. I was surrendered to Him in this moment. He is my ultimate source of authority. This heaviness was preventing His authority from being revealed in this area. I represented His authority and needed to enforce it. I knew what I had to do.

Very quietly, but distinctly I addressed the spiritual force in operation disturbing these people.

 "I know you can hear me," I whispered as Zaka continued preaching to utter chaos.

"I know you are trying to disrupt us. I represent Jesus Christ the King of Kings and Lord of Lords who is the Lord of Madagascar and the Lord of this village.." Zaka was getting frustrated too.

"I command you in Jesus name to stop disrupting this meeting. Leave these people alone in the authority of Jesus name."

No one in the village or among my team members heard the prayer. Yet, I sensed that unseen spiritual forces had. Almost immediately the dogs turned around and went back into the forest. The angry women turned and parted ways. The kids sat quietly on the grass as if nothing had ever been the matter, and the young men disappeared.

The contrast couldn't have been more pronounced. Zaka found his rhythm and the anointing flowed powerfully. A few moments later he gave the altar call and hundreds of people raised their hands to receive Christ. He looked around very proud of himself as I continued kneeling in the dirt.

Prayer and the enforcement of Christ's authority made all the difference that day.

Question of the Day: Are you walking in Christ's authority today? Why or why not? How can you more fully experience Christ's authority in your life?

Musings: There are so many things that could be said about this story that I think are relevant to our spiritual maturity. First, the real victories are fought and won on our knees long before they manifest in the natural.

Second, true spiritual authority has nothing to do with volume, shouting, or yelling. Either we have it or we don't and no amount of human activity can ever compensate for divine unction. Third, Christ's authority must be enforced through His people—the church.

Fourth, the enemy will resist, hinder, thwart, obstruct, and confound the people of God as they try to advance the purposes of God. Fifth, and finally, appropriating Christ's authority over the forces of darkness will produce glorious victories.

I have meditated on Christ's authority often since this moment. Has Christ's authority diminished at any point in the past 2000 years? Of course not. It remains a constant truth in every generation. He is Lord. He is King. So where is the critical issue? I believe it is the measure of our heart's surrender to Jesus' Lordship.

Someone once said, *"If He's not Lord of all; He's not Lord at all."* I first heard that statement many years ago in my high school years. It used to convict me because I lived a lifestyle of Christian compromise. Jesus was Lord only when it was convenient to me. Secret areas of sin dominated my heart making it nearly impossible to take any ground from the forces of darkness.

It's very difficult to fight against something that has an open door into our hearts. It just doesn't work. It's ludicrous actually. The spiritual principle is that spiritual authority is found in the place of genuine surrender. When we give ourselves fully to Christ and His will, He will give us a full measure of Himself as well as His authority.

I've tried advancing the Kingdom with compromise in my life—it's so empty and such an exercise in futility. By contrast, when we walk in the full measure of His authority God works with us in tremendous ways.

Conclusion

To conclude volume two we return to the powerful stanza from CT Studd's poem quoted in volume 1. The story goes that he found a wadded up piece of paper on the ground that contained the now popular lines that he incorporated into his poem.

These two lines shook the young university student with the reality of eternity. At the time he was one of the most famous cricket players in all of England. Yet, he realized that his life had very little eternal impact. He lived for fame and pleasure. God so gripped his heart that he almost immediately gave up his popularity to pursue a missionary assignment in the nation of China.

For me, his decision and corresponding action must not be glossed over. An athlete of national import decides that if his life would have eternal significance for Christ there is only one thing to be done—he must give himself wholly to the cause of missions.

One life will soon be past
Only what's done for Christ will last.

His heart was gripped with the sudden awareness of God's Mission and he responded by connecting his life to missions. The point for us in the 21st century is simply this, are the things we are living for now significant in the light of eternity? This is no casual question. It is weighty demanding much inner searching to identify our values and corresponding actions. I don't think that everyone reading this book is called to immediately sell everything and move to some obscure corner of planet earth. Rather, I think that all of us must continually seek to connect to Heaven's Mission and make our lives count for eternity.

How we respond to this challenge is between Jesus and our hearts. In other words, no one can dictate this to us. I think it looks different for different people. Yet, I can state with 100% certainty that everyone is called to connect to Heaven's Mission through the avenue of missions. There aren't any exemptions to the Great Commission. It isn't for a select group of disciples with a global sort of worldview. Missions is a must.

There have been seasons in my life when I haven't been able to be actively involved in the missions fields of East Africa that I know and love. In these seasons prayer— both individual as well as the mobilization of corporate prayer have played a critical role.

Finances have been instrumental in this regard too. I have never made a lot of money in my life, but I sure have given it away to missions causes and endeavors. The amazing thing has been to watch as God has increased my capacity to give. I started giving $25 monthly in college. The Lord increased my capacity to $50 a month. Then it wasn't long before He challenged me to do $100. I felt the prompting to increase again. Then, $400. Then $600. You get the idea.

This notion of stagnant giving speaks to me of stagnant faith. We know the will of God. He wants the nations to come into the Kingdom of His Son, Jesus Christ. In order for this to happen Paul tell us in Romans 10 that a preacher must be sent so that the word can be communicated and faith released into people's hearts. Sending the communicator of God's Word requires resources. The more communicators that are sent, the more resources will be required. Obviously, the world is a big place requiring many more communicators. Hence, there is still a need for more resources.

What I have learned is that God has the resources—He's just looking for someone that will be obedient to connect His resources with His will. When faith and giving, particularly in the area of missions, collide anything can happen!

Finally, beyond prayer and giving, there is another great way to connect with missions when unable to move to another country. America is the most diverse nation on planet earth. People live in the United States from just about every corner of the globe. When I lived in Springfield, Missouri I had the privilege of leading an Indian grad student and a Rwandan undergraduate student to Christ. When I lived in Tulsa I had the privilege of leading a Mexican waitress and an Angolan

English as a Second Language student to Christ. My friends included several Turks, a couple of Syrians, multiple Indians, a Bangladeshi, Ethiopians, etc.. America is amazingly diverse. People are usually much more open in the States as well.

To my African friends reading this book. The same is true for you. You are called to connect with God's heart for missions. The hour of letting the mzungu be the face of missions is gone. In Nairobi, there are Somalis, Sudanese, Ethiopians, Indians, and Eritreans. In Dar, there are Zanzibaris, Pembalese, Indians, Somalis, just to name a few. The nations are congregating in the capital cities of the world. I believe that it is a kairos moment for reaching the nations with the message of Jesus Christ.

My prayer is that the people of God would respond like never before to this challenge. May this be the generation that reaches the nations!

33097178R00091

Made in the USA
San Bernardino, CA
24 April 2016